Everything you need to know about

WINE

JONATHAN RAY

ILLUSTRATIONS BY EMILY HARE

Everything you need to know about

WINE

JONATHAN RAY

ILLUSTRATIONS BY EMILY HARE

BURFORD BOOKS

For
E.M.R. and E.M.R.
with love

Everything you need to know about wine
by Jonathan Ray.

First published in the United States in 1999 by
Burford Books Inc, 32 Morris Avenue, Springfield
NJ 07081.

Library of Congress Cataloging-in Publication Data
Ray, Jonathon.
Everything you need to know about wine/Jonathon
Ray: illustrations by Emily Hare.
p.cm.
Includes index.
ISBN 1-58080-041-6 (pbk.)
1. Wine and winemaking. I. Title
TP548.R286 1999   99-16959
641.2'2--dc21   CIP

Commissioning Editor: Rebecca Spry
Managing Editor: Hilary Lumsden
Design: Miranda Harvey
Editor: Jamie Ambrose
Illustrations: Emily Hare
Production: Karen Farquhar
Index: Anne Barrett

Typeset in M Perpetua, Syntax and Gill Sans.

Printed and bound by Toppan Printing Company in
China.

Acknowledgments
I would like to thank Hattie Ellis for her
matchmaking skills; Emily Hare for her sublime
illustrations; Rebecca Spry and Hilary Lumsden for
their hard work and refreshing sense of fun; Judith
Murray for her encouragement; David Roberts MW,
of Berry Bros and Rudd, for his generous expertise;
and my wife, Marina, for her uncomplaining, selfless
support and excellent advice.

CONTENTS

6 Introduction

7 Classifications

8 France

24 Germany

30 Italy

40 Spain

48 Portugal

52 Rest of Europe

62 United States and Canada

70 South America

76 Africa

80 Australia & New Zealand

88 Madeira, port & sherry

94 Red grapes

108 White grapes

120 Living with wine

126 Wine with food

132 Wine glossary

142 Hangover cures

144 Index

how to use this book

INTRODUCTION

Let's say that you know how to drive a car – how to change gear, steer, reverse and so on. I bet you don't know how the internal combustion engine works. Does this matter? Of course not. You still know how to use the car and get enjoyment from it.

Why should wine be any different? Some kind soul has made a bottle of wine. You don't need to know how he or she did it; you just need to know how best to enjoy the wine. If you want to find out which wine to drink with dinner or what an unfamiliar label means without wading through a morass of technical information, then this is the book for you.

The following pages will introduce you to the world's key winemaking regions and grape varieties, give advice on how to store wine, how and when to serve it and with what dishes. They will not explain the importance of *terroir*, debate the merits of oak-ageing or analyse microclimates.

Everything you need to know about wine is an introductory guide for those who want to enjoy wine, not pass an exam. Having said that, plenty of course work is required, because the best way to learn more about this wonderful subject is to taste wines for yourself.

So if you want to learn how to choose the perfect wine in a restaurant or at home with your in-laws, read on, and more importantly, enjoy, because this book is for you.

BOTTLE SHAPES
The shape of a wine bottle is a useful, but not infallible, guide to its contents. The following illustrations show the five classic bottle shapes.

1 Port and Madeira.

2 Bordeaux and wines made from the classic Bordeaux grapes – Cabernet Sauvignon, Merlot, Sémillon and Sauvignon Blanc – from other regions.

3 Alsace and other aromatic white wines, especially from Germany.

4 Champagne and sparkling wines.

5 Burgundy and wines made from the classic Burgundy grapes – Chardonnay and Pinot Noir – from other regions.

1   2   3   4   5

CLASSIFICATIONS

FRANCE French wine laws split the country's wines into four categories.

The largest and (theoretically) the best is *Appellation d'Origine Contrôlée* (AOC or AC). The AC guarantees that a wine comes from where the label says it does, is made from approved grapes and is produced in an approved way.

Next down is *Vin Délimité de Qualité Supérieure* (VDQS), which has similar controls, but for regions that are not classified as AC.

The next step down is *Vin de Pays*, country wine, which states on the label where the wine is from and (sometimes) the grapes from which it is made. Finally comes *Vin de Table*, table wine, which can be made from practically any grapes, grown practically anywhere.

GERMANY The top wine grade is *Qualitätswein mit Prädikat* (QmP), which must be made without the addition of sugar. QmP is based on how ripe the grapes used to make the wine were when picked. The six ripeness categories, from dry to sweet, are:
Kabinett from ripe grapes in a dry style;
Spätlese from late-picked, extra ripe grapes;
Auslese from specially selected bunches of very ripe (sometimes nobly rotten) grapes;
Beerenauslese (BA) from individually selected, extra-ripe, nobly rotten grapes;
Trockenbeerenauslese (TBA) from dried, specially selected, nobly rotten single grapes;

Eiswein: from ripe grapes left to freeze on the vine. Ice crystals in the grape concentrate the sugar in the juice.

The next grade down, *Qualitätswein bestimmter Anbaugebiete* (QbA), is, in theory at least, better than *Landwein* and *Deutscher Tafelwein* (German table wine). *Landwein* is a step up from *Deutscher Tafelwein,* which is made from a blend of grapes with added sugar. *Deutscher* means that the grapes are grown in Germany – plain *Tafelwein* can come from anywhere in the EU.

ITALY The *Denominazione di Origine Controllata* (DOC) is Italy's answer to France's AC system. The DOC specifies which grapes may be used in which sites and determines minimum alcohol levels, but does not guarantee quality.

The *Denominazione di Origine Controllata e Garantita* (DOCG) is a stricter set of rules guaranteeing a wine's origins and (to an extent) its quality. *Vino da Tavola* (VdT), or table wine, is officially the lowest of the low. Yet many wines that do not fit into the DOC framework are among Italy's finest wines. New laws forbid VdTs from stating their origins, grape varieties and vintages, so many former superior VdTs now fall under the *Indicazione Geografica Tipica* (IGT) category, equal to the French *Vin de Pays*.

See country entries for other wine laws.

france

ALSACE

IN A NUTSHELL A grossly underrated region producing superb, elegant, spicy white wines.

GEOGRAPHY Northeastern France, between the River Rhine and the Vosges Mountains.

WINES AND GRAPES Single varietals are made from and named after the following grapes: Gewurztraminer (spelt here without the umlaut), Muscat, Pinot Blanc, Pinot Gris, Riesling, Sylvaner and Pinot Noir. Chasselas is used in some blended wines, but these tend to be fairly ordinary. Most wine bears the Alsace AC, but the best wines (theoretically at least) may be labelled *grand cru*.

QUALITY Alsace wines are among the most delicious in France, with each grape being easily identified on the nose and palate. The words *vendange tardive* (late-harvest) on an Alsace label usually mean that the wine has a sweeter style. More rare is *sélection des grains nobles,* which indicates that the wine is fabulously sweet and is made only when the grapes develop botrytis.

WHITES These include dry, faintly aromatic Sylvaner and Pinot Blanc; rich, petrolly Riesling; intensely grapey yet dry Muscat; smoky, spicy, creamy Pinot Gris; and the almost overpoweringly spicy Gewurztraminer.

REDS Pinot Noir is surprisingly successful here, but is rarely exported. It is generally light and perfumed, but oakier versions do exist.

SPARKLING WINES Sparkling Crémant d'Alsace is a joy.

WINE AND FOOD Lighter whites, including Muscat and Pinot Blanc, go well with fish or poultry. Pinot Gris can take the place of many reds at a meal. Gewurztraminer goes well with spicy food and, when late-picked, is ideal with *foie gras* or pungent cheeses. Pinot Noir is the perfect foil for Alsace specialities such as *choucroute*.

RECOMMENDED PRODUCERS INCLUDE J Becker, Léon Beyer, Blanck, Cave Vinicole de Turckheim, Dopff & Irion, Dopff au Moulin, Rolly Gassmann, Hugel, Josmeyer, André Kientzler, Kreydenweiss, Kuentz-Bas, Gustave Lorentz, Schlumberger, Schoffit, Pierre Sparr, FE Trimbach, Willm and Zind-Humbrecht.

RECOMMENDED VINTAGES INCLUDE 1985, 1988, 1989, 1990, 1992, 1993, 1994, 1995, 1996, 1997.

TRIVIA The wines of the region are known as "Alsace" wines rather than "Alsatian" wines; an alsatian is a dog.

BORDEAUX

IN A NUTSHELL Bordeaux is the world's most famous fine wine-producing region, making red wines (known as claret) of stunning complexity and sweet white wines with a depth of flavour that few areas can equal. Bordeaux also produces fine dry white wines.

GEOGRAPHY The region sits either side of the River Gironde in southwest France. The main wine districts in Bordeaux are Pomerol, St-Emilion, Graves and Pessac-Léognan, Sauternes and Barsac, and the Médoc.

WINES AND GRAPES Red wines make up three-quarters of Bordeaux's wine production and most of them are blends. Five grapes may be used to make claret: Cabernet Sauvignon, Merlot, Cabernet Franc, Malbec and Petit Verdot. Cabernet Sauvignon is the dominant red grape in all areas except for St-Emilion and Pomerol, where soil and climate favour Merlot. No two clarets are the same, with minute differences between the *châteaux* in soil, microclimate and blending techniques leading to enormous differences in the resulting wines.

QUALITY Bordeaux is strictly governed by the *Appellation Contrôlée* laws. The most basic quality is Bordeaux AC. Bordeaux Supérieur AC is slightly better quality, with higher minimum levels of alcohol. If the label mentions a district, such as St-Emilion or the Médoc, the wine should be of higher quality still. On top of these are wines which mention specific

villages or communes, such as Pauillac or St-Julien in the Médoc.

In addition, the top *châteaux* of the Médoc (and one from the Graves – Château Haut-Brion) have their own classification system, established in 1855. These top *châteaux* are classified as *crus classés*, which are sub-divided into five ranks, ranging from *premier cru* (first growth) down to *cinquième cru* (fifth growth). Below these main categories are *cru bourgeois* wines.

In the 1950s, the wines of St-Emilion were also classified into three ranks (*premier grand cru classé*, *grand cru classé* and *grand cru*).

WHITES The great dry white wines from **Graves** and **Pessac-Léognan** are made from Sauvignon Blanc and Sémillon, as are the dessert wines of **Sauternes** and **Barsac**, but for these the grapes are affected by botrytis. Also look out for good whites from **Entre-Deux-Mers**.

REDS Within the Médoc are the *communes* Pauillac, Margaux, St-Julien and St-Estèphe. **Pauillac** boasts three of the five first growths and is regarded by many as the best *commune*. **Margaux**'s wines are regularly praised for their grace and elegant silkiness. **St-Julien** is the smallest of the four main *communes* and probably makes the most fragrant and best-value wines. **St-Estèphe**, meanwhile, is arguably the least well-regarded, although it still produces some great wines that are noted for their high levels of tannin.

Outside the Médoc, **Graves** and **Pessac-Léognan** produce fine red wines which tend to be earthier than those of the Médoc. Tiny **Pomerol** and **St-Emilion** both base their wines on Merlot and Cabernet Franc. Their wines are noted for their softness and elegance, being more approachable when young than the wines of the Médoc. St-Emilion also has several satellite *communes* which include "St-Emilion" in their names and which produce cheaper wines that are similar to St-Emilion in style but that inevitably have far less finesse.

Look out for Merlot-based reds from **Fronsac** and good reds from **Entre-Deux-Mers**, **Côtes de Castillon** and **Premières Côtes de Bordeaux**.

SWEET WINES The great dessert wines of **Sauternes** and **Barsac** are made from botrytis-affected Sémillon with some Sauvignon Blanc and Muscadelle. Barsacs tend to be slightly lighter than Sauternes and, just to be awkward, they are entitled to call themselves Sauternes (although Sauternes cannot call themselves Barsacs). The sweet wines of **Ste-Croix-du-Mont** don't have the depth of flavour of Sauternes or Barsac, but they are still delightful and considerably cheaper.

WINE AND FOOD Claret goes with any red meat, poultry or cheese. The Bordelais often drink powerfully sweet Sauternes at the start of a meal with a rich pâté as well as at the end with blue cheese or more pudding.

RECOMMENDED PRODUCERS INCLUDE (all *châteaux*)
Pessac-Léognan: de Fieuzal, Haut-Bailly and Haut-Brion.
Margaux: d'Angludet, Brane-Cantenac, Margaux and Palmer.
Médoc/Haut-Médoc: Cantemerle, Chasse-Spleen, Cissac and Liversan.
Pauillac: Batailley, Haut-Bages-Monpelou, Lafite-Rothschild, Latour, Lynch-Bages and Mouton-Rothschild.
Pomerol: Beauregard, L'Evangile, Gazin, Pétrus, le Pin and Vieux-Château-Certan.
St-Emilion: Figeac, Fombrauge, Clos Fourtet, Canon La Gaffelière and Larmande.
St-Estèphe: Beau-Site and Le Crock.
St-Julien: Gruaud-Larose, Langoa-Barton, Léoville-Barton and Talbot.
Sauternes and **Barsac:** Climens, Doisy-Daëne, de Malle, Rieussec and d'Yquem.

RECOMMENDED VINTAGES INCLUDE 1961, 1966, 1970, 1978, 1982, 1983, 1985, 1986, 1988, 1989, 1990, 1995, 1996.

TRIVIA Bordeaux produces about 750 million bottles of wine a year.

IN A NUTSHELL Burgundy produces some of the finest wines in the world – and some of the most expensive.

GEOGRAPHY A region in eastern France which, for wine purposes, runs south from Chablis in the Yonne to Lyon and is divided into the following areas: Beaujolais, Chablis, the Côte d'Or (comprising the Côte de Nuits and the Côte de Beaune), the Côte Chalonnaise and the Mâconnais.

WINES AND GRAPES Most red burgundy is made from Pinot Noir and most white burgundy from Chardonnay, although there are exceptions, including Beaujolais, which is made from Gamay.

QUALITY The wines of Burgundy are divided into five quality categories which are, from top to bottom: *grand cru*, *premier cru*, *appellation communale*, specific district appellations and simple Bourgogne.

However, just because the bottle of wine in your hand is from the same village and vintage as the one you drank last night doesn't mean that it is of the same quality. It may have come from a poorer site or have been made by one of any number of wine-growers. In Burgundy, the name of the producer or *négoçiant* (merchant-shipper) is crucial, and it is well worth finding and memorising ones that you like. This knowledge is only gained from experience, but as the wines are often outstanding that shouldn't be a hardship.

WHITES In the **Côte de Beaune**, whites of the highest quality include Meursault, Puligny-Montrachet and Corton-Charlemagne – long-lasting wines of great power and finesse. The **Côte Chalonnaise** produces reliable white wines such as Montagny and Rully. The **Mâconnais** yields good-quality whites such as Pouilly-Fuissé, St-Véran and Mâcon-Lugny.

CHABLIS This wine deserves a special mention because of its popularity and unique style. Some say that it is Chardonnay at its finest, with an elegant, slightly nervy, steely, minerally tang.

Chablis is divided into four quality levels, with seven Chablis *grands crus* at the top, followed by Chablis *premier cru*, Chablis and Petit Chablis. If a wine isn't from Chablis, then it has no right to the name.

At its most basic, Chablis is light, dry and clean. At its best (for example, *grands crus* Les Clos, Les Preuses and Valmur or *premiers crus* Fourchaume, Côte de Léchet, Mont de Milieu and Montée de Tonnerre), it ranks among the finest white wines in the world.

REDS The northern **Côte de Nuits** produces the longest-lasting red wines in Burgundy, such as Gevrey-Chambertin and Morey-St-Denis, while a little further south such celebrated names as Nuits-St-Georges and Vosne-Romanée can be found. Generally speaking, the **Côte de Beaune** produces reds of high quality, including Pommard, Volnay, Beaune, Aloxe-Corton and Pernand-

Vergelesses. The **Côte Chalonnaise** yields decent red wines for early drinking, such as Mercurey, Rully and Givry.

BEAUJOLAIS The popularity and availability of Beaujolais make it worthy of a special mention. Whatever its quality level, Beaujolais should be light and fruity with a high gluggability factor.

Beaujolais is made up of 39 villages, 10 of which have *cru* status, being allowed to sell their wine under their village names: Brouilly, Chénas, Chiroubles, Côte de Brouilly, Fleurie, Juliénas, Morgon, Moulin-à-Vent, Regnié and St-Amour.

Beaujolais Nouveau is wine from the latest vintage, released at midnight on the third Wednesday in November. At its best it is light, zesty and refreshing. At its worst? Cook with it.

WINE AND FOOD Lesser white burgundies make good *apéritifs* or partners to light fish dishes, while the grandest go well with turbot or scallops. Mighty red burgundies cry out for *boeuf bourguignon, coq au vin* or game dishes such as jugged hare and roast pheasant. Beaujolais is delicious chilled and goes well with cold meats and picnics, while Chablis partners oysters and other seafood, smoked salmon, sushi or chicken.

RECOMMENDED PRODUCERS INCLUDE Bouchard Père et Fils, Doudet-Naudin, Joseph Drouhin, J Faiveley, Jaffelin Frères, Louis Jadot, Louis Latour, Leroy, Méo-Camuzet, Domaine de la Romanée-Conti, T Moillard, Prosper-Maufoux and Antonin Rodet.

Beaujolais: Château de la Chaize, Charvet, A Colonge, Georges Duboeuf, Echallier, Jacky Janodet, Metrat, R Sarrau, Château des Tours and Trichard.

Chablis: the La Chablisienne co-operative, Jean-Paul Droin, Joseph Drouhin, William Fèvre, Louis Michel, J Moreau and Albert Pic.

RECOMMENDED VINTAGES INCLUDE *reds* 1985, 1988, 1989, 1990, 1992; *whites* 1985, 1986, 1988, 1989, 1990, 1992, 1995, 1996, 1997; *Beaujolais* 1994, 1995, 1997.

TRIVIA In 1395, Philip the Bold outlawed Gamay from Burgundy (what *had* it done?), decreeing that it might be grown only in Beaujolais, where it has flourished ever since.

CHAMPAGNE

IN A NUTSHELL For most people, champagne is unquestionably the finest of all sparkling wines.

GEOGRAPHY Champagne comes from the northernmost vineyards in France, in the valley of the River Marne, centred round the towns of Epernay and Reims. Only wines from the designated area of Champagne may be called champagne.

WINES AND GRAPES Champagne may only be made from Chardonnay (white), Pinot Noir and Pinot Meunier (both red). *Blanc de blancs* champagne is made entirely from Chardonnay; *blanc de noirs* entirely from the red grapes. Rosé champagne is the only quality rosé wine in Europe that is allowed to be a blend of red and white wines.

In Champagne, climate, soil, grapes and the method of production combine magically to produce a sparkling wine that is unlike that from anywhere else. Similar wines are made elsewhere from the same grapes using the same method (known outside Champagne as *méthode traditionelle*), but they never quite manage to upstage champagne.

QUALITY To make champagne, winemakers encourage a second fermentation to occur in the bottle by adding yeast and sugar to the wine. Most champagne is non-vintage (NV), with wines from different vintages being blended in such a way as to ensure consistency in each producer's distinctive house style. Vintage champagne is made only in the best years from only the best grapes; it must contain 80 per cent of grapes from that vintage and be aged for at least three years before being released onto the market. The best wines a Champagne house produces, in theory at least, are called *prestige cuvées*.

STYLES *Extra brut* is the driest style of champagne. *Brut* varies from dry to very dry. Despite its name, *extra sec* or "extra dry" is less dry than *brut*, *sec* is less dry again, *demi-sec* is medium-sweet and *doux* is the sweetest of all.

WINE AND FOOD Chilled champagne makes a fine *apéritif* and can be drunk with a meal.

RECOMMENDED PRODUCERS INCLUDE Billecart-Salmon, Bollinger, Canard-Duchêne, Cattier, Duval-Leroy, Gosset, Gratien, Charles Heidsieck, Krug, Lanson, Laurent-Perrier, Möet et Chandon, Mumm, Perrier-Jouët, Philipponnat, Piper-Heidsieck, Pol Roger, Pommery, Louis Roederer, Ruinart, Salon, Taittinger and Veuve Clicquot.

RECOMMENDED VINTAGES INCLUDE 1975, 1976, 1979, 1982, 1983, 1985, 1986, 1988, 1989, 1990.

TRIVIA A wine merchant was to send a case of Mumm to a lady on her wedding day. Fresh out of Mumm, he sent Veuve Clicquot instead, not realising that the accompanying note read: "I hope you will be one soon" – a charming sentiment sent with Mumm, but not with Veuve Clicquot, popularly known as "the Widow".

LOIRE

IN A NUTSHELL The vineyards of the Loire Valley stretch for almost 1,000 kilometres and produce a wide variety of wines. On the whole they are white, dry and refreshing, but reds, sparklers and sweet wines are also made.

GEOGRAPHY The Loire runs from the heart of France just east of Orléans, westwards to the Atlantic coast, and includes the wine regions of Pays Nantais, Anjou and Touraine.

WINES AND GRAPES The Loire is most famous for its white wines, the best being made from Sauvignon Blanc or Chenin Blanc. The region also produces fine sparkling wines and a few light reds made mainly from Cabernet Franc.

Wine names in the Loire can be confusing. For example, Pouilly-Fumé is the name given to wines made from Sauvignon Blanc in and around the town of Pouilly-sur-Loire, while Pouilly-sur-Loire is the name given to wines of the area made from the Chasselas grape. Neither wine has anything to do with Pouilly-Fuissé, a white burgundy made from Chardonnay. Meanwhile, Muscadet is not a place but a grape variety (also known as Melon de Bourgogne), not to be confused with a different variety called Muscadelle. (You may want to read that paragraph again slowly.)

QUALITY White wines are the main players, and the Sauvignon Blanc and Chenin Blanc grapes stand out.

WHITE AND SWEET WINES **Sancerre** and **Pouilly-Fumé** are arguably the finest Sauvignon Blancs in the world. Most are not for keeping, part of their attraction being their youthful zing.

Basic **Muscadet** should be light and easy to drink; **Muscadet de Sèvre-et-Maine** may be yeasty and biscuity or even honeyed; **Muscadet des Coteaux de la Loire** falls between the previous two; and since 1995 there has been a fourth Muscadet, **Muscadet Côtes de Grand Lieu**. Whatever its AC, Muscadet is at its best when allowed to sit on its lees (the yeasty sludge left over after fermentation), during which time it picks up deeper flavours and sometimes a slight spritz. These wines, labelled "Muscadet Sur Lie", are the ones to go for.

Good white **Anjou** and **Touraine** are steely and honeyed, **Coteaux du Layon** can be sweet or semi-sweet, while **Savennières** makes an excellent dry white wine.

Vouvray, made from Chenin Blanc, can be dry, semi-sweet, sweet, still or sparkling. The best sweet Vouvrays are utterly delicious, with Chenin Blanc's acidity cutting through the botrytis-enhanced sweetness to produce wines that are less unctuous than the dessert wines of Sauternes and that can last for decades.

Keep an eye out, too, for the pleasant, good-value Sauvignon Blancs from **Quincy**, **Reuilly** and **Menetou-Salon**.

REDS AND ROSÉS The rosé **Cabernet d'Anjou** is made from Cabernet Franc, as are the delightfully fresh and fruity **Chinon**

and **Bourgeuil** red wines, which are not dissimilar in style to Beaujolais. In fact, like Beaujolais, these wines are particularly seductive when lightly chilled and drunk young, although they do have the capacity to age. Bourgeuil is usually the slightly fuller of the two. Red **Saumur** and **Saumur-Champigny** are also made from Cabernet Franc, while light, refreshing red and rosé **Sancerres** are made from Pinot Noir.

SPARKLING WINES The best sparkling **Vouvray** wines are good value for money. Sparkling **Saumur** is also well worth sampling. Although many Champagne houses own vineyards here, the wines don't have the finesse of champagne, mainly because the grapes used – Chenin Blanc and Cabernet Franc – just aren't as good at the job as Chardonnay and Pinot Noir.

WINE AND FOOD Loire wines can accompany almost everything. Sparkling Saumurs and Vouvrays make fine *apéritifs*. Muscadet is ideal with seafood, while Pouilly-Fumé and Sancerre are perfect with fish dishes. Bourgeuil, Chinon and red Sancerre go well with meat or salads, while sweet Coteaux du Layons or sweet Vouvrays are equally successful with strong cheeses or puddings.

RECOMMENDED PRODUCERS INCLUDE
Bourgeuil: Domaine de la Grive and Pierre-Jacques Druet.
Chinon: Couly-Dutheil, Charles Joguet and Olga Raffault.

Menetou-Salon: Domaine de Châtenoy and Henry Pellé.
Muscadet: Donatien Bahuaud, Guy Bossard, Domaine du Chasseloir, Château de Cléray/Sauvion et Fils, Chéreau-Carré, Pierre Luneau, Château de Goulaine and Louis Métaireau.
Pouilly-Fumé and **Sancerre:** Lucien Crochet, Didier Dagueneau, André Dezat, Gitton Père et Fils, de Ladoucette (Château du Nozet), Alphonse Mellot, Henri Natter, Pabiot, Château de Tracy, Domaine Vacheron, André Vatan and Edmond Vatan.
Quincy: Jacques Rouzé.
Reuilly: Henry Beurdin and Claude Lafond.
Saumur: Bouvet-Ladubay, Domaine Filliatreau, Gratien et Meyer and Langlois-Chateau.
Savennières: Domaine des Baumard, Château de Chamboureau (Yves Soulez), Clos de la Coulée de Serrant (Nicolas Joly) and Domaines aux Moines.
Vouvray: Marc Brédif, Didier Champalou, Clos Naudin, Foreau, Château Gaudrelle, Huët and Château de Moncontour.

RECOMMENDED VINTAGES INCLUDE 1985, 1988, 1989, 1990, 1993, 1995, 1996.

PROVENCE

IN A NUTSHELL Provence is one of the most rapidly improving wine regions in France, with a revitalised industry producing many good, but often expensive, wines.

GEOGRAPHY Provence is in the most southeastern corner of France, surrounding the city of Toulon, southeast of the Rhône.

WINES AND GRAPES The reds are big and full-bodied and very Rhône-like. The rosés are good, dry and herby, while the whites are, um, not always brilliant. A wide selection of grape varieties is used.

QUALITY Spurred on by the successes of the New World, many producers are tearing up the rule book and starting again. Investment, new grape varieties and so-called "flying winemakers" from the New World are changing the traditional industry dramatically.

Although much of Provence's wine is a disappointment (great glugged on holiday, grim at home), there have always been some goodies, and from now on there are going to be more. Not only is the quality of the wines improving, but the new ones are being marketed in a more user-friendly way, with grape varieties often listed on the label.

WHITES, REDS AND ROSÉS Some of the best wines in Provence come from **Bandol**, the reds and rosés of which (in order to qualify for AC status) must contain at least 50 per cent Mourvèdre, with Grenache, Cinsault and Syrah making up the rest. The

wines are aged in wood for at least 18 months, after which they usually need plenty of bottle age. A tiny amount of anonymous white wine is also made, usually from Clairette, Ugni Blanc, Bourboulenc and Sauvignon Blanc.

Côtes de Provence is the largest AC in Provence, producing mainly rosés which, like the reds, are made from Cabernet Sauvignon, Grenache, Cinsault, Mourvèdre, Syrah and others. The quality is variable, but improving.

Cassis (not to be confused with the blackcurrant cordial crème de cassis) makes mainly light, dry whites from Ugni Blanc, Clairette, Marsanne and Sauvignon Blanc, although there are some drinkable reds and rosés.

Other regions to note include **Coteaux d'Aix-en-Provence**, **Palette** and **Bellet**.

WINE AND FOOD The reds make good partners for hearty fare and *charcouterie*. The whites go well with anchovies and other seafood. The rosés are great for seductions.

RECOMMENDED PRODUCERS INCLUDE Domaine Bernarde, Domaine Champagna, Domaine des Féraud, Domaines Ott, Château Pigoudet, Château Pradeaux, Domaine Richeaume, Château Simone, Domaine Tempier, Domaine de Trévallon, Château de Val-Joanis and Château Vignelaure.

RECOMMENDED VINTAGES INCLUDE 1986, 1988, 1989, 1990, 1995.

TRIVIA Winemaking has taken place in Provence since around 600BC.

# RHONE (NORTHERN)

IN A NUTSHELL The northern Rhône's hefty, full-bodied red wines are in great demand.

GEOGRAPHY South along the Rhône Valley from Vienne, just south of Lyon, to Valence.

WINES AND GRAPES Syrah is top dog here, producing such mighty red wines as Hermitage, Crozes-Hermitage, Côte-Rôtie and Cornas. Whites are made from Viognier or from the Marsanne-Roussanne double act.

QUALITY Reds are the main players: rich, heady, full of tannin and in need of plenty of ageing. The best are comparable in quality to fine Bordeaux, and are considerably cheaper.

WHITES Hermitage is made from Marsanne and Roussanne; it can be sullen and dull when young, but with age gains a softer, richer personality. **Condrieu** is dry, elegant, rich and spicy, made from Viognier. **Château-Grillet**, another pure Viognier white, is made just south of the Condrieu AC, and is expensive, rare and can be overrated (unless you find it at its perfumed best). **St-Péray**, to the south, offers still and sparkling white wines.

REDS Hermitage is full-bodied, with a spicy ripeness and loads of raspberry/blackberry fruit. A dash of Marsanne and Roussanne is allowed to soften the big Syrah edges, but it may need up to 15 years to mature. **Crozes-Hermitage** is a smoky, less butch version of Hermitage. **St-Joseph** is lighter and smoother, but still offers a fair whack of

fruit. In **Côte-Rôtie**, 20 per cent Viognier added to Syrah results in rich, spicy, perfumed wines that are softer than Hermitage. **Cornas** is a pure Syrah stonker in a tarry overcoat.

WINE AND FOOD Reds go with game dishes, whites with chicken or fish.

RECOMMENDED PRODUCERS INCLUDE
Condrieu: Y Cuilleron, Dumazet, Guigal, A Perret and G Vernay.
Cornas: T Allemand, G de Barjac, Clape, J-L Colombo, Marcel Juge, R Michel and A Voge.
Côte-Rôtie: Burgaud, Gilles Barge, Champet, Delas Frères, Dervieux-Thaize, Guigal, Paul Jaboulet-Aîné, Joseph Jamet, Jasmin, Rostaing and Vidal-Fleury.
Crozes-Hermitage: Cave des Clairmonts, Château de Curson, Delas Frères, Domaine des Entrefaux, Guigal and Paul Jaboulet-Aîné.
Hermitage: Chapoutier, Chave, Clape, Delas Frères, Desmeure, B Faurie, Grippat, Guigal, Paul Jaboulet-Aîné, Sorrel and de Vallouit.
St-Joseph: Chave, Pierre Coursodon and JL Grippat and Paul Jaboulet-Aîné.

RECOMMENDED VINTAGES INCLUDE *reds* 1978, 1980, 1982, 1985, 1986, 1988, 1989, 1990, 1991, 1994, 1995; *whites* 1978, 1982, 1983, 1987, 1988, 1989, 1990, 1991, 1996.

TRIVIA Legend has it that Hermitage is named after a 13th century crusader who lived as a hermit on the hill above Tain l'Hermitage.

RHONE (SOUTHERN)

IN A NUTSHELL The warm climate results in big, mainly red, alcoholic wines.

GEOGRAPHY From Montélimar south almost to Avignon.

WINES AND GRAPES The red wines of the southern Rhône are made predominantly from Grenache, bolstered by a touch of Syrah and other grape varieties. Although big, beefy and alcoholic, they are softer than the wines of their northern neighbours.

QUALITY Many more wines are made than in the northern Rhône, but fewer great ones.

WHITES White **Châteauneuf-du-Pape** can be found, but it is much rarer than red. **Lirac** whites are lighter than those of Châteauneuf-du-Pape.

REDS AND ROSÉS The area's most famous red wine is **Châteauneuf-du-Pape**, which is considered to be among the world's finest wines. 13 grape varieties are permitted in its Grenache-dominated blend, which produces big, generous, fruitily spicy wines which are softer than the wines of the northern Rhône.
  As well as rosés, **Gigondas** produces powerful, earthy reds. Red **Vacqueyras** is equally robust, but slightly more refined. **Lirac** reds are lighter than those of Châteauneuf; with Lirac rosés, they represent some of the area's best value. **Tavel** makes rosé of variable quality, but at best it is full and refreshing due to the high Grenache content.

Also look out for the red wines of **Côtes du Ventoux**, **Côtes du Rhône**, **Côtes du Rhône-Villages** and **Coteaux du Tricastin**.

FORTIFIED WINES The *Vin Doux Naturel* **Muscat de Beaumes-de-Venise** is a fine alternative to Sauternes.

WINE AND FOOD Reds go well with roasts and casseroles, rosés with poultry, whites with salads, *Vins Doux Naturels* with desserts.

RECOMMENDED PRODUCERS INCLUDE
Châteauneuf-du-Pape: Château de Beaucastel, H Bonneau, Les Cailloux, Domaine Chante-Cigale, Château Fortia, Domaine de la Janasse, Château la Nerthe, Clos des Papes, Château Rayas and Domaine du Vieux Télégraphe.
Côtes du Rhône/Rhône-Villages: Paul Jaboulet-Aîné, Guigal, Domaine Rabasse-Charavin and Domain Ste-Anne.
Gigondas: Domaine du Cayron, Domaine St-Gayan, Domaine Goubert and Château Raspail-Aÿ.
Muscat de Beaumes-de-Venise: Domaine de Coyeux and Domaine Durban.

RECOMMENDED VINTAGES INCLUDE 1981, 1983, 1985, 1986, 1988, 1989, 1990, 1993, 1994, 1995, 1998.

TRIVIA Châteauneuf-du-Pape means "new castle of the pope": a reference to the palace built here by Pope John XXII in the 14th century.

SOUTHERN FRANCE

IN A NUTSHELL Best known for gallons of cheap plonk, southern France is at last producing some fascinating country wines.

GEOGRAPHY Languedoc-Roussillon stretches from Montpellier to beyond Perpignon, and covers the Aude, Gard, Hérault and Pyrénées-Orientales *départements*.

WINES AND GRAPES Much of the wine is basic, but improvement has been discernible. Traditional reds are made from Syrah, Grenache and Mourvèdre, often blended with less well-known grapes. Excellent *Vins de Pays* (particularly *Vins de Pays d'Oc*) are now being made from Cabernet Sauvignon or Chardonnay.

QUALITY Spurred on by New World competition, fine modern wines are emerging, often marketed under the name of the grape.

WHITE, RED, ROSÉ AND SPARKLING WINES Big, full-bodied red wines are made in **Corbières** and **Minervois** from spicy blends of Carignan, Cinsault, Grenache, Mourvèdre and Syrah. Lighter, fruitier and plummier examples come from **Faugères** and **St-Chinian**. **Coteaux du Languedoc** reds have been improving for years; recently, the whites have caught up with them. Some deliciously juicy red and rosé **Côtes du Roussillons** and **Côtes du Roussillon-Villages** are also being made, though not in quite the same quality scale. **Fitou** is a generous, old-style red wine based on Carignan. **Blanquette de Limoux** is a very good sparkling wine based on Mauzac (also known as Blanquette) and blended with Chardonnay and Chenin Blanc.

FORTIFIED WINES The region has fine *Vins Doux Naturels* in the form of **Muscat de Frontignan**, **Muscat de Mireval**, **Muscat de Rivesaltes** and **Banyuls**, a delicious port-like oddity.

WINE AND FOOD The still wines are suited to Mediterranean dishes, such as plainly grilled fish, ratatouille, *bouillabaise* and roast peppers.

RECOMMENDED PRODUCERS INCLUDE Domaine de l'Aigle, Château Aiguilloux, Domaine des Amouries, Domaine de la Baume, Château de Beauregard, Château le Bouis, Domaine Capiou, Château de Calissanne, Caraguilhes, Domaine de Cazeneuve, Domaine de Fontsainte, Fortant de France, Château de Gourgazaud, Château Haut-Fabrèges, James Herrick, Domaine de l'Hortus, Château de Jau, Domaine des Jougla, Château Lascaux, Château de Lastours, Mas Brugière, Mas de Daumas Gassac, Mas Jullien, Mas Morties, Mont Tauch, Jean-Pierre Ormières, Les Palais, Château Pech-Céleyran, Pierre Petit, La Serre, Jean de Thelin, Vidal-Gaillard and Domaine Virginie.

RECOMMENDED VINTAGES INCLUDE 1988, 1989, 1990, 1991, 1993, 1994, 1995, 1998.

TRIVIA Hérault has more vines planted than any other *département* in France.

SOUTHWEST FRANCE, JURA AND SAVOIE

IN A NUTSHELL As prices have risen elsewhere, so has the popularity of these regional wines.

GEOGRAPHY Southwest France: east from Bordeaux towards Bergerac and south towards the Spanish border. Jura and Savoie: between Burgundy and the Swiss and Italian borders.

WINES AND GRAPES Wines from the southwest are mainly in the Bordeaux style; from Jura and Savoie they're chiefly white.

QUALITY Good value can be found in the red and white wines of Bergerac and Buzet. The wines of Jura and Savoie are rarely exported.

SOUTHWEST WHITE, RED AND SWEET WINES The reds and whites of **Bergerac** and **Buzet** are made from the same grapes as those used in Bordeaux. These wines often compare well in quality with the *petits châteaux* and are cheaper. At its best, Bergerac's botrytis-affected Monbazillac is almost as good as Sauternes. The "black" wines of **Cahors** are so-called because of their tannins and deep colour; made from Malbec blended with Merlot and Tannat, they are lighter and more approachable in style than they once were. **Gaillac** comes in all colours, but the whites and slightly sparkling Perlé are the best known. **Madiran** is a tannic red wine based on Tannat. **Jurançon** is a curious dry, medium or sweet white wine. Decent Sauvignon Blanc-based whites come from **Côtes de Duras**, and reds come from **Côtes du Frontonnais**. **Vins de Pays des Côtes de Gascogne** are fresh whites.

JURA AND SAVOIE WHITES AND REDS Three-quarters of Savoie's wines are white and most are made from Jacquère, Chasselas and Roussette. The best is the crisp **Roussette de Savoie**. Decent light reds are made from Gamay and Pinot Noir, and there are refreshing white sparklers. Jura is famous for *Vin Jaune*, a dry sherry-like wine made from Savagnin and aged for six years in cask.

WINE AND FOOD Whites are great for picnics, Bergerac reds for bangers and mash.

RECOMMENDED PRODUCERS INCLUDE
Bergerac: Château Court-les-Mûts, Château de la Jaubertie and Château de Panisseau.
Buzet: Domaine Padère, Château Pierron and Caves Réunis des Côtes de Buzet.
Cahors: Château de Cayrou, Château de Chambert, Clos Triguedina, Château de Haute-Serre and Domaine des Savarines.
VdP des Côtes de Gascogne: Grassa, Plaimont and Domaine du Tariquet.
Gaillac: J Albert, J Auque, Boissel-Rhodes, Domaine J Cros and Labastide de Lévis.
Jura: Château d'Arlay and Reverchon et Fils.
Jurançon: Domaine Cauhapé and Domaine Jolys.
Monbazillac: Château de la Jaubertie
Savoie: P Boniface and Varichon et Clerc.

RECOMMENDED VINTAGES INCLUDE 1983, 1985, 1986, 1988, 1989, 1990, 1995.

TRIVIA For some reason, Jura's *Vin Jaune* is always bottled in clavelins of precisely 62cl.

germany

MOSEL-SAAR-RUWER

IN A NUTSHELL Wines from the Mosel-Saar-Ruwer are lighter and crisper than many other German wines, and are sold in green bottles.

GEOGRAPHY Vineyards are found along the length of the River Mosel and its tributaries the Saar and the Ruwer, stretching from Germany's borders with Luxembourg and France in the southwest to Koblenz in the northeast.

WINES AND GRAPES Only white wines are made here, mainly from Riesling and Müller-Thurgau. Other grape varieties are being planted; Weissburgunder (Pinot Blanc) in particular is on the increase.

QUALITY The Mosel-Saar-Ruwer is one of Germany's 13 *anbaugebiete* (designated wine-producing regions), the River Mosel passing steep, slatey slopes covered with some of Germany's most famous vineyards.

WHITES These are richly fragrant, pale and light-bodied, with a lively, fruity, acidity. Riesling of great elegance grows on the steep, south-facing slopes of the Mosel, especially around **Wiltingen** and **Scharzhofberg** in the **Saar-Ruwer** district, and in the **Mittelmosel** (Middle Mosel) district round **Bernkastel**, **Piesport**,

Wehlen, **Brauneberg**, **Graach**, **Zeltingen** and **Erden**.

Although Riesling accounts for half the vineyard area, Müller-Thurgau is also widely planted, often at the expense of Riesling. If a wine doesn't state a grape variety on its label, it is likely to have been made from (or partly made from) Müller-Thurgau.

WINE AND FOOD Mosel-Saar-Ruwer wines are great drunk on their own. However, Mosel Riesling Kabinett goes well with local veal dishes or smoked fish, while Weissburgunders make ideal partners for freshwater fish.

RECOMMENDED PRODUCERS INCLUDE JJ Christoffel, Egon Müller zu Scharzhof, Grans-Fassian, Fritz Haag, Reinhold Haart, Karthäuserhof, Heribert Kerpen, J Lauerburg, Dr Loosen, Maximin Grünhaus, Reichsgraf von Kesselstatt, JP Reinert, Max Ferd Richter, Willi Schaefer and Selbach-Oster.

RECOMMENDED VINTAGES INCLUDE 1971, 1976, 1983, 1985, 1988, 1989, 1990, 1992, 1993, 1994, 1995, 1996, 1997.

TRIVIA The wine cellars of the Bischöfliche Weingüter in Trier are so large that the cellarmaster travels through them by bicycle.

THE RHINE

IN A NUTSHELL Rhine wines (which come in brown bottles) are represented at their worst by the original mass-produced alcopop, Liebfraumilch, and at their best by some of the finest, most elegant and fragrant white wines that money can buy.

GEOGRAPHY The Rhine wine regions run south from Bonn to Wissembourg on the French border.

WINES AND GRAPES White wines are still the mainstay here: Rieslings of amazing purity are probably the most famous. There are white wines made from the likes of Huxelrebe, Silvaner, Gewürztraminer, Müller-Thurgau, Grauburgunder, Weissburgunder and Scheurebe. Surprisingly, good Pinot Noirs (here known as Spätburgunders) are also produced.

QUALITY The Rhine incorporates the six *anbaugebiete* (designated wine-producing regions) of the Ahr, Mittelrhein, Rheingau, Nahe, Rheinhessen and Pfalz.

WHITE, SWEET AND SPARKLING WINES The **Rheingau** is the most famous of Germany's *anbaugebiete*. It stretches from just east of Hochheim (the village that inspired the British to coin the word "Hock" for the region's wines) to Lorch, near the Mittelrhein. The Rheingau is one long hillside forming just one district, Bereich Johannisberg. Riesling is the major player here, grown only on the best sites and yielding noble, elegant wines characterised by a refined, spicy fragrance, fruity acidity and rich ripeness of flavour.

Bacharach is the most important village in the **Mittelrhein**, and here high-quality wines are made from Riesling (which accounts for three-quarters of the vineyard area), Müller-Thurgau and Kerner. Good sekt (sparkling wine) is also made.

The **Nahe**, a small region west of Rheinhessen and east of the Mosel, takes its name from a tributary of the Rhine. Although Müller-Thurgau is the most planted variety, Riesling is grown in the better areas. The wines have the elegance of Rheingau wines and the flowery bouquet of Mosel wines, together with a minerally quality that is all their own.

The **Rheinhessen**, which lies in a valley bordered by the Nahe in the west and the Rhine in the north and east, is the largest of the wine-producing regions, with production second only to that of the Pfalz. Nierstein, just south of Mainz, is the Rheinhessen's most famous wine-growing community, but its fame led to many an inferior "Niersteiner" being made in an effort to exploit what was once a high-quality wine. Many grape varieties are planted here, especially Riesling, Silvaner, Müller-Thurgau and several new crossings. Good wines are made in the region, but to the Rheinhessen's eternal shame, half of its 12-million-cases-a-year production is Liebfraumilch.

The **Pfalz** (formerly the Rheinpfalz), is Germany's second-largest wine region.

Bordered by Rheinhessen in the north and France in the south and west, the vineyards run for some 50 miles. The northern half of the region in particular is home to many top vineyards. The villages of **Wachenheim**, **Forst**, **Deidesheim** and **Ruppertsberg** are well known for a variety of white (and red) wines, including spicy Gewürztraminers, elegant, dry Rieslings and lush Scheurebe dessert wines.

Finally, Riesling and the ubiquitous Müller-Thurgau are produced in the **Ahr**, but most of these wines are drunk locally.

REDS Strangely enough for a generally white wine-producing area, 85 per cent of the **Ahr**'s vineyards are devoted to red grapes, even though this tiny region is one of the most northern in Germany. Spätburgunder and Portugieser yield fruity reds here.

Good Spätburgunder is also made in the **Rheingau**, near the town of Assmannshausen. In the **Rheinhessen**, Portugieser is the most important red grape, although the area around Ingelheim is known for its full-bodied Spätburgunders. In the **Pfalz**, smooth, classy, fruit-filled reds are made from Spätburgunder, while Dornfelder yields attractive reds made for everyday drinking.

WINE AND FOOD The finest German wines are best drunk on their own in order to appreciate their true delicacy, although they obviously make the best partners for the local cuisine.

RECOMMENDED PRODUCERS INCLUDE
Ahr: Kreuzberg and Meyer-Näkel.
Mittelrhein: Toni Jost and Randolph Kauer.
Nahe: Crusius, H Dönnhoff, Krüger-Rumpf, Adolf Lotzbeyer, Prinz zu Salm-Dalberg, Reichsgraf von Plettenberg and Schlossgut Diel.
Pfalz: Dr Ludwig von Basserman-Jordan, Dr Bürklin-Wolf, Kurt Darting, Koehler-Ruprecht, Lingenfelder, Herbert Messmer, Müller-Catoir, Klaus Neckerauer, Pfeffingen and Reichsrat von Buhl.
Rheingau: JB Becker, Georg Breuer, Domdechant Werner, August Eser, Freiherr zu Knyphausen, Geheimrat J Wegeler Erben (Deinhard), Johannishof, August Kesseler, Franz Künstler, Josef Leitz, Schloss Johannisberg, Schloss Reinhartshausen, Schloss Schönbron and Robert Weil.
Rheinhessen: Baumann, Brüder Dr Becker, Freiherr Heyl zu Herrnsheim, Gunderloch, Guntrum, Georg Albrecht Schneider, Heinrich Seebrich and Carl Sittman.

RECOMMENDED VINTAGES INCLUDE 1985, 1988, 1989, 1990, 1992, 1993, 1994.

TRIVIA Notoriously, the Rheinhessen is the birthplace of Liebfraumilch, originally made from grapes grown in vineyards surrounding the Liebfrauenkirche (the Church of Our Lady) in Worms.

REST OF GERMANY

IN A NUTSHELL These regions provide a wider range of styles than either the Rhine or the Mosel, albeit not of such high quality.

GEOGRAPHY South to the Bodensee (Lake Constance) and east to Dresden.

WINES AND GRAPES The wines are more varied than those of the rest of Germany, and include dry Pinot Blancs, gentle rosés and fruity Pinot Noirs.

QUALITY The region has six *anbaugebiete*: Franken, Württemberg, Hessische Bergstrasse, Baden, Sachsen and Saale-Unstrut.

WHITES Franken is the most interesting of the regions, and its wines are considered to be the most "masculine" in Germany; they are often drier and earthier than those of other regions. The best of Franken's wines are made from Silvaner and the slightly less fine wines from Müller-Thurgau and Bacchus.
   Württemberg produces vigorous white wines from Riesling, Müller-Thurgau, Kerner and Silvaner, but most of them are consumed locally. **Hessische Bergstrasse** concentrates on Riesling, making fragrant, rich wines with more body but less acidity and finesse than those of the Rheingau. **Baden** is Germany's southernmost wine region and one of its largest, running from Heidelberg in the north to the Bodensee in the south. The grapes planted include Gewürztraminer and Riesling. **Sachsen** (the smallest of Germany's wine regions) and **Saale-Unstrut** were once part

of East Germany; most of their wines are made from Müller-Thurgau and need to improve before they are seen abroad more often.

REDS Württemberg is the largest red wine-producing region in the country. Half of the region's vineyards are planted with red grapes such as Lemberger (Austria's Blaufränkisch), Trollinger and Samtrot, but few of these fruity reds are exported. A quarter of **Baden**'s vineyards are planted with Spätburgunder, most of which is used to make the rosé Spätburgunder Weissherbst.

WINE AND FOOD The whites suit crab, grilled fish and mild cheeses, and a BLT has no better partner than a Württemberg Spätburgunder.

RECOMMENDED PRODUCERS INCLUDE
Baden: Bercher, Dr Heger, Karl-Heinz Johner and Wolf Metternich.
Franken: Fürstlich Castell'sches Domänenamt, Juliusspital, Ernst Popp and Hans Wirsching.
Saale-Unstrut: Lützkendorf.
Sachsen: Schloss Proschwitz, Jan Ulrich and Klaus Zimmerling.
Württemberg: Graf Adelmann, Fürst zu Hohenlohe-Oehringen and Graf von Neipperg.

RECOMMENDED VINTAGES INCLUDE 1971, 1976, 1983, 1985, 1988, 1989, 1990, 1992, 1993, 1994.

TRIVIA Most Franken wines are bottled in a squat, green flagon called a *Bocksbeutal*, said to be modelled on the scrotum of a goat.

italy

CENTRAL ITALY

IN A NUTSHELL Central Italy is the home of such well-known wines as Chianti, Brunello di Montalcino, Vino Nobile di Montepulciano, Orvieto, Frascati, Lambrusco, Verdicchio and Montepulciano d'Abruzzo.

GEOGRAPHY The region includes Tuscany, Umbria, Latium and the Marches, among others.

WINES AND GRAPES Sangiovese is the most significant grape in the Chianti blend, while Cabernet Sauvignon has taken on an important role in the production of "Super Tuscans".

QUALITY Italy is the world's most productive winemaking country, and its regions are diverse. There are over 1,000 grapes (many have different names in different parts of the country), and the industry is governed by wine laws which are sometimes ignored (*see* page seven). Sadly the country's wines lurch between brilliant and awful, and by the time you discover what you've got it's too late.

In wine terms, Tuscany is the most significant region in central Italy. It includes the five DOCGs of Chianti, Brunello di Montalcino, Carmignano, Vino Nobile di Montepulciano and Vernaccia di San Gimignano.

TUSCAN WHITES Tuscany's most famous white wine is **Vernaccia di San Gimignano**, which is smooth and nutty and dates back to the 13th century. Gold, rich and full-bodied, the wine's oxidised character makes it an acquired taste.

TUSCAN REDS Chianti veers alarmingly between stonker and stinker. Chianti proper is made in eight sub-zones, wines from which can be called Chianti or can take the name of the sub-zone, too. Wine from outside a sub-zone, but from within the broad Chianti area, are called simply Chianti. **Chianti Classico** is best, and can be recognised by a black cockerel on the label. *Riserva* on the label means that the wine has been aged for three years before release. Made from at least 90 per cent Sangiovese, good Chianti should taste of fresh herbs and cherries, but bad Chianti is about as bad as wine can get.

Some winemakers found that adding Cabernet Sauvignon, Merlot or Shiraz to their wines improved them no end. However, producers were forbidden to call the resulting wines Chianti because they were made from grapes not approved by DOC regulations. Consequently, producers were obliged to class their wines *Vini da Tavola*, but these experimental wines became so good that they were nick-named **"Super Tuscans"**, much to the annoyance of the authorities. Famous "Super Tuscans" include Sassicaia (subsequently granted its own DOC in 1994), Ornellaia, Solaia and Tignanello.

Other reds include **Brunello di Montalcino** and **Rosso di Montalcino**: big, dark wines with plenty of tannin and structure. Brunello is a clone of Sangiovese and these wines age well. Confusingly, **Vino Nobile di Montepulciano** is not made from the grape Montepulciano, but named after the town; its grapes are Prugnolo (Sangiovese) and Canaiolo, with up to 20 per cent other varieties. **Rosso di Montepulciano**, from the same grapes, isn't aged for as long.

OTHER TUSCAN WINES The sherry-like *Vin Santo* can be red or white, sweet or dry, and is made from Malvasia, Trebbiano or Grechetto, the grapes being dried on mats before vinification. The wine is aged for three to 10 years and has orange peel, nutty flavours.

OTHER REGIONS Umbria's main red grapes are Sangiovese, Canaiolo and Sagrantino. **Montefalco** is a good-quality red wine made from Sangiovese, Trebbiano and Sagrantino (and the sweet Montefalco Sagrantino is worth a detour). The **Torgiano** DOC and DOCG offer good white and red wines. **Oriveto** is one of **Umbria**'s most notable whites; it can be dry, medium or sweet.

Rome is the hub of **Latium**, where 90 per cent of production is white. **Frascati** is the region's most famous wine, but it suffers from severe variations in quality. All too often it is dull, but the good stuff can be fresh. The white **Est! Est!! Est!!!** has a certain fame, mainly because of its daft but historic name.

Elsewhere in central Italy, **Emilia-Romagna** produces the lightly fizzy **Lambrusco** – sweet or dry; red, white or pink. Most is produced in bulk for the export market and is of dubious quality, but if the wine bears a DOC (from Sorbara, say) it can be exciting. Fresh white **Verdicchio** is the big attraction in the **Marches**, while **Abruzzi** is justly famous for its rich, juicy red **Montepulciano d'Abruzzo**.

WINE AND FOOD "Super Tuscans" need something special to accompany them, but the rest of the region's wines are happiest with homemade Italian food or takeaway pizza.

RECOMMENDED PRODUCERS INCLUDE Emilia-Romagna: Cavicchioli, Cesari, Fattoria Paradiso, Vallania, Vallunga and Zerbina. **Marches/Abruzzo:** Garofoli, Illuminati, Sartarelli, Umani Ronchi and Valentini. **Tuscany:** Altesino, Antinori, Argiano, Avignonesi, Biondi-Santi, Boscarelli, Caparzo, Capezzana, Castellare, Castello di Ama, Castello di Brolio, Castello di Cacchiano, Castello dei Rampolla, Eredi Fuligni, Falchini, Felsina-Berardenga, Fontodi, Frescobaldi, Isole e Olena, Monsanto, Monte Vertine, Montellori, Nittardi, Nozzole, Panaretta, Poggio Antico, Tenuta Il Poggione, Ricasoli, Ruffino, San Felice, Verrazzano and Vignamaggio. **Umbria/Latium:** Adanti, Antinori, Bigi, Colle Picchioni, Fontana Candida and Lungarotti.

RECOMMENDED VINTAGES INCLUDE 1985, 1988, 1989, 1990, 1991, 1993, 1994, 1995.

TRIVIA Chianti was the first wine region to have its boundaries and production controlled by law.

NORTHEAST ITALY

IN A NUTSHELL The best-known wines from northeast Italy are those staples of wine bars and bistros the world over: Vapolicella, Bardolino and Soave.

GEOGRAPHY This area of Italy runs to the Swiss border, encompassing the wine-growing regions of the Veneto, Friuli-Venezia Giulia and Trentino-Alto Adige.

It is worth remembering that the Alto Adige (the northern half of the Trentino-Alto Adige region) is often known as the Südtirol and was once part of Austria, a fact which is reflected in the Germanic names of the grape varieties and producers.

WINES AND GRAPES Local grapes rub shoulders with "international" varieties to make light reds, crisp whites and exotic late-picked wines that can be sweet or dry.

QUALITY As with the rest of Italy, quality in the northeast varies greatly. That said, the Veneto is Italy's top producer of DOC wines, accounting for over the fifth of the country's DOC production.

VENETO WHITES The wines of **Soave** can be dreadful, but look hard and good examples can be found: they should be rich and fresh, with lemony fruit, nuts and a creamy texture. Made from Garganega and Trebbiano, Soave is best when from the *classico* area. Soave *Supériore* must have a one per cent minimum higher alcohol level than *classico* and must have been aged for at least eight months.

Since 1992, Chardonnay has been permitted in Soave wines in an effort to liven them up.

Prosecco is a sparkling, medium-sweet or dry wine made from the grape of the same name, and it makes a splendid *apéritif*. **Bianco di Custoza** is a highly drinkable dry white wine which is similar to Soave.

VENETO REDS AND ROSÉS The best-known wines in the **Veneto** are Bardolino and Valpolicella, which can both be ghastly or delicious. Bardolino should be soft and light, while Valpolicella should be a bit heavier, with fragrant cherry-like fruit.

Valpolicella is made mainly from Corvina, Rondinella and Molinara, the best wines being labelled *classico*, meaning that they come from the inner and better zone in the DOC area. Those labelled *supériore* must have a 12 per cent minimum alcohol level and must have been aged for at least a year.

Bardolino is made from the same grape varieties as Valpolicella but is lighter and fruitier; again, *classico* and *supériore* wines are the best. Bardolino Chiaretto is a refreshing rosé that often outshines the mainstream red.

OTHER REGIONS' WHITES Nearly all the wines of the **Alto Adige** area of Trentino-Alto Adige are sold under the name of a single grape variety. The best whites are made from Chardonnay (oaked and unoaked), Muscat, Gewürztraminer, Pinot Grigio, Pinot Bianco, Müller-Thurgau and Riesling. There is also oodles of forgettable sparkling wine from Chardonnay, Pinot Grigio and Pinot Bianco.

Friuli-Venezia Giulia grows more than 70 grape varieties, the main white grape of which is Tocai, not to be confused with other Tokays. Other varieties include Chardonnay, Pinot Bianco and Sauvignon Blanc.

OTHER REGIONS' REDS AND ROSÉS The southern half of Trentino-Alto Adige around **Trentino** makes good reds from Teroldego, Cabernet Sauvignon, Merlot and Pinot Noir. Decent rosés are also made. In **Friuli-Venezia Giulia** the main red is Refosco and there is some Cabernet Sauvignon, Cabernet Franc, Merlot and Pinot Nero.

SWEET WINES **Recioto,** a speciality of **Veneto**, is a sweet wine that can be made from red or white grapes which are partially dried to concentrate their sugars before gentle fermentation occurs to reach the highest level of alcohol possible (about 16 per cent) without fortification. **Recioto di Soave** is delightfully sweet, while **Recioto della Valpolicella** can be *amabile* (sweet) or *amarone* (dry); the latter style is an extraordinary wine of intense depth.

WINE AND FOOD Drink Italian wines with Italian dishes. All the whites will go well with pasta-based dishes and Recioto di Soave is ideal with Tiramisú.

RECOMMENDED PRODUCERS INCLUDE **Alto Adige:** Gray, Franz Haas, Hofstätter, Alois Lageder, Santa Margherita, Tiefenbrunner.

Friuli-Venezia Giulia: Bidoli, Borgo del Tiglio, Collavini, Dorigo, Dri, Marco Felluga, Gravner, Jermann, Puiatti and Schioppetto.
Trentino: Ca'Vit, Conti Martini, Fedrigotti, Foradori, Guerrieri-Gonzaga, Maso Poli, Pojer & Sandri and Vinicola Aldeno.
Veneto: Allegrini, Anselmi, Bertani, Boscaini, Brigaldara, Conte Loredan, Gasparini, Guerrieri-Rizzardi, Maculan, Masi, Pieropan, Quintarelli, Tedeschi, Le Ragose, Romano Dal Forno, La Salette, Santa Margherita and Santa Sofia.

RECOMMENDED VINTAGES INCLUDE 1985, 1986, 1988, 1989, 1990, 1993, 1994, 1995.

TRIVIA In Harry's Bar in Venice, local Prosecco is used in place of champagne to make the delightfully refreshing Bellini cocktail. So far, no one has complained.

NORTHWEST ITALY

IN A NUTSHELL The region is dominated by the province of Piemonte (Piedmont to English-speakers) province.

GEOGRAPHY Northwest Italy means Piemonte to most wine-lovers, and "Piemonte" means literally "mountain foot" – not surprising, really, as the region lies at the bottom of the Alps.

WINES AND GRAPES Nebbiolo is the main grape in the northwest, making big, butch reds such as Barolo and Barbaresco, while the Barbera and Dolcetto grapes take supporting roles. Muscat is used to make Moscato d'Asti and Asti.

QUALITY Piemonte produces what some consider to be Italy's two finest wines, Barolo and Barbaresco, as well as the country's best-known sparkling wine, Asti.

PIEMONTE WHITE AND SPARKLING WINES **Asti**, now a separate DOCG which tries hard to avoid the former label of Asti Spumante, is Italy's most famous sparkling wine. At its best, Asti is a delicious, unpretentious sweet or semi-sweet wine. A similar wine, **Moscato d'Asti**, is also produced in Piemonte, and is marginally less fizzy and alcoholic. It is easy to make fun of these wines, but on the right occasion they can be charming.

Gavi is the main white wine of note in Piemonte; made from the Cortese grape, it is dry and creamy with hints of apple.

PIEMONTE REDS The most celebrated Piemonte wine is **Barolo**. Possibly Italy's finest contribution to the wine world, this muscular red (made from Nebbiolo, of course) must be aged for three years, two of which must be spent in wood. *Riserve* require four years ageing and *riserve speciali*, five. The wines have a strength of over 13 per cent alcohol and tend to be expensive.

Barbaresco, also made from Nebbiolo, is lighter, softer and less alcoholic than Barolo. It is aged for only two years (one of which is spent in wood), although *riserva* is aged for three years and *riserva speciale* for four. The best Barbarescos are rich, spicy and dry with an elusive sweetness, and are usually considered more elegant than Barolo but less robust and long-lived. In these wines Nebbiolo combines tannin and perfume like no other grape variety on earth. Both wines are named after villages – a common practice in Italy.

Another notable red is **Spanna** (which is another name for Nebbiolo and so immediately puts paid to the idea that all Italian wines are named after locations). Piemonte is awash with other attractive Nebbiolo-based reds, including **Gattinara** and **Ghemme**, while Barbera accounts for **Barbera d'Asti**, **Barbera d'Alba** and **Barbera del Monferrato**. The Dolcetto grape makes soft, plummy, chocolatey reds, such as **Dolcetto d'Alba** and **Dolcetto di Dogliani**.

OTHER REGIONS **Lombardy**, which has Milan as its capital, produces a lot of wine from 13 DOC areas, but few of these wines are of great importance. A fragrant Soave-like white wine called **Lugana** is worth seeking out, as are the still white wines (Pinot Bianco/Chardonnay blends), pleasant reds and slightly sparkling whites and rosés from the **Franciacorta** DOC.

Liguria is a little known region tucked between Provence and Tuscany, whose best red is a fruity, Beaujolais-like wine called Rossese di Dolceacqua. Ligurian white wines include the crisp and citrus-like **Vermentino** and the fuller-bodied, peachy **Pigato**.

The tiny French-speaking **Valle d'Aosta** is Italy's smallest wine-growing region, producing reds, whites and rosés from vineyards planted on steep Alpine slopes. Of the approved grape varieties, Nebbiolo is the most widely planted red grape, supplemented by small amounts of Gamay and Pinot Noir. Müller-Thurgau and Pinot Grigio are the most popular whites.

WINE AND FOOD Barolo and Barbaresco go well with game, heavily sauced pasta dishes and risottos.

RECOMMENDED PRODUCERS INCLUDE
Liguria: Riccardo Bruna, Cascina du Feipú and Lupi.
Lombardy: Guido Berlucchi, Ca'del Bosco, Ca'dei Frati, Longhi de Carli, Tenuta Mazzolino and Visconti.
Piemonte: Abbazia di Vallechiara, Alasia,
Elio Altare, Matteo Ascheri, Bava, Braida, Borgogno, Cascina la Barbatella, Castello di Neive, Cavallotto, Ceretto, Domenico Clerico, Aldo Conterno, Giacomo Conterno, Duca d'Asti, Fontanafredda, Gaja, Bruno Giacosa, Elio Grasso, Moccagatta, Parusso, Pio Cesare, Pira, Alfredo Prunotto, Renato Ratti, Rocche dei Manzoni, Luciano Sandrone, Paul Scavino and Vietti.
Valle d'Aosta: Charrière et Fils, La Grotta de Vegneron, and Ezio Voyat.

RECOMMENDED VINTAGES INCLUDE 1978, 1982, 1983, 1985, 1986, 1988, 1989, 1990, 1996.

TRIVIA Barolo is supposedly "the wine of kings and the king of wines" – according to Barolo producers, of course.

SOUTHERN ITALY

IN A NUTSHELL Although southern Italy is remarkably productive, there are few wines of note and the region is greatly overshadowed by others in Italy.

GEOGRAPHY Southern Italy for the wine-lover consists of Basilicata, Calabria, Campania, Apulia, Sicily and Sardinia: all hot and, in winemaking terms, primitive.

WINES AND GRAPES Big reds made from Aglianico, smoky, dry white and sweet wines made from Greco, and Sicily's once-prized fortified wine, Marsala, are the highlights of the region.

QUALITY Southern Italy is very much the poor cousin of Italy's wine regions. Plenty of wine is made, but little is of serious quality, with the exception of one or two local curiosities and Marsala which, sadly, has long since fallen out of fashion.

WHITE, RED, ROSÉ AND SPARKLING WINES
Apulia (or Puglia), in the heel of Italy, is the south's best region. Although it makes huge amounts of wine (its annual production is greater than that of Germany), Apulia still lags behind Sicily as the most productive region in Italy. Red grapes account for four-fifths of the region's production, and much of that is made into vermouth or blending wine for the rest of the country. The main red grapes are Primitivo (thought to be a relative of Zinfandel), Negroamaro, Malvasia Nera and Uva di Troia. White grapes include Verdeca, Bianca d'Alessano, Bombino Bianco (great name!), Malvasia Bianca and Trebbiano (Ugni Blanc).

Modern technology is finding its way here (as are winemakers from the New World), and decent reds and rosés are being made at last. Castel del Monte is one name to look out for as a producer of highly regarded red wines made from Uva di Troia, Aglianico, Montepulciano, Pinot Nero (Pinot Noir) and Sangiovese; the rosés, too, are good, but the whites are rather dull. Taurino also makes good wines in the Salice Salentino DOC. Some classic varieties are also grown here.

Naples and Salerno lie in the region of **Campania**, which is in something of the doldrums. Here, old-fashioned techniques produce good, but far from great, reds, whites and rosés. The main red grape is Aglianico, which has been grown here since the 7th century BC. The region produces red wines that are noted for their tannins and flavours of tar and chocolate, the best of which are the hefty wines of **Taurasi** DOCG, in which Aglianico is blended with up to 30 per cent Barbera, Piedrosso and Sangiovese. Other wines of the region to look out for include the reds, whites and rosés called Lacryma Christi del Vesuvio, and the white Greco di Tufo, which can either be dry or sweetly sparkling.

Calabria is a traditional (polite word for old-fashioned) and mountainous region set in the toe of Italy, whose better wines are based on the white Greco and the red Gaglioppo grapes. Cirò is Calabria's best-known red wine, made from the aforementioned Gaglioppo, and was allegedly reserved by the ancient Greeks for Olympic champions. A peachy, smoky white, Cirò is also made from Greco and Trebbiano, and a rosé version springs from these two grapes blended with Gaglioppo. Calabria's antiquated technology is gradually giving way to modern machinery and methods; considering the region's potential, this can only be a good thing.

Basilicata is a barren area, with only one wine of note: the thick, chocolate-touched, spicy red Aglianico del Vulture.

There are plenty of grape varieties in **Sicily**, Italy's most productive region in terms of size and acreage under vine. Most of the production is distilled, but there are red and white *Vini da Tavola*, including the delicious Duca di Salaparuta and the Terre di Ginestra wines.

Sardinia's wines are getting better (well, they couldn't get much worse). The white wines are fairly drinkable, if nondescript, and there are some drinkable reds made from Cannonau, a local type of Grenache.

SWEET AND FORTIFIED WINES **Sicily's** finest wine is **Marsala**, a once highly regarded fortified wine which has been made here since Roman times. In the late 1700s, an Englishman named John Woodhouse devised the techniques for making Marsala and pioneered the wine's popularity in England. Much of Marsala's flavour comes from the oxidisation that takes place during ageing. It can be dry, medium or sweet, although all wines are originally made dry and must reach 12 per cent alcohol. Also look out for the luscious dessert wine, **Greco di Bianco**, made from the Greco grape in **Calabria**.

WINE AND FOOD The reds and whites of the region should be drunk on a quayside in the sun with whatever is the *trattoria's* dish of the day.

RECOMMENDED PRODUCERS INCLUDE
Apulia: Azienda Nuova Murgia, Leone de Castris, Rivera, Castel del Monte, Cosimo Taurino, Torrevento and Le Trulle.
Basilicata: D'Angelo.
Calabria: Ceratti and Librandi.
Campania: Mastroberardino, Struzziero and Vignadora.
Sardinia: Antonio Argiolas and Sella & Mosca.
Sicily: Calatrasi, Corvo, De Bartoli, Donnafugata, Florio, Hauner, Regaleali and Settesoli.

RECOMMENDED VINTAGES INCLUDE 1981, 1982, 1983, 1985, 1986, 1988, 1990, 1992, 1994.

TRIVIA Campania's Lacryma (or Lacrima) Christi del Vesuvio translates as "The Tears of Christ of Vesuvius". Although what Jesus was doing on Vesuvio, no-one knows.

1	Rías Baixas	12	Valdepeñas
2	Toro	13	La Mancha
3	Rueda	14	Utiel-Requena
4	Ribera del Duero	15	Valencia
5	Rioja	16	Jumilla
6	Navarra	17	Yecla
7	Somontano	18	Jerez
8	Cariñena	19	Montilla-Moriles
9	Priorato	20	Málaga
10	Tarragona	21	Extremadura
11	Penedès		

spain

CATALONIA

IN A NUTSHELL Catalonia's reputation rests mainly on its Cava and the international style red and white wines of Penedès.

GEOGRAPHY The wine-growing regions run south from France and both west and east from Barcelona on the Mediterranean coast.

WINES AND GRAPES Catalonia has both ancient and modern wine styles, from basic co-op fare made from local grapes, to exciting wines made from the likes of Cabernet Sauvignon, Merlot and Chardonnay.

QUALITY From highest to lowest, Spain's wine classifications are: *Denominación de Origen Calificada* (DOCa) for superior DOs; *Denominación de Origen* (DO), which specifies source, grape varieties and production methods; *Vino de la Tierra*, which is similar to French *Vin de Pays*; *Vino Comarcal*, for wine showing some regional character; and *Vino de Mesa*, which can be of good quality.

WHITES AND REDS The still wines of **Penedès** owe their success to mavericks such as Miguel Torres and Jean León, whose foresight has resulted in good-quality whites made from Chardonnay and Sauvignon Blanc, and reds, made from Cabernet, Merlot, Tempranillo and other traditional varieties.

Priorato has planted more international grapes, and its wines are improving. **Costers del Segre**'s many co-ops yield sound reds from Merlot, Cabernet Sauvignon and Tempranillo, as well as good whites. **Conca de Barberà** has decent whites from Chardonnay, Parellada and Macabeo. **Alella** makes some quite good dry and semi-sweet whites.

SPARKLING AND SWEET WINES Penedès is famous for Cava, which can be excellent, although its a blend of Parellada, Macabeo and Xarel-lo grapes gives it a taste that is not always suited to the export market. **Costers del Segre** makes some decent Cava and **Conca de Barberà** has some sparkling wines to offer too. There are a few good dessert wines in **Tarragona**.

WINE AND FOOD The best Cavas make good *apéritifs*, while Penedès reds and whites from Torres *et al* will partner many a meal.

RECOMMENDED PRODUCERS INCLUDE Cava: Castellblanch, Codorníu, CoViDes, Freixenet, Marqués de Monistrol and Raïmat. **Penedès:** CoViDes, Jean León, Marqués de Monistrol, Mascaró, Masía Bach, Puig Roca, Raventós i Blanc and Miguel Torres.

RECOMMENDED VINTAGES INCLUDE 1982, 1985, 1987, 1991, 1994, 1995.

CENTRAL SPAIN

IN A NUTSHELL A large chunk of Spain which makes plenty of quaffable wines.

GEOGRAPHY The central part of Spain, including the arid plain of La Mancha, Valdepeñas, Utiel-Requena, Madrid and Méntrida.

WINES AND GRAPES The wines range from hefty reds to rosés and whites. The main grapes are Cencibel (Tempranillo) and Airén, with some Macabeo, Chardonnay, Cabernet Sauvignon and Merlot. But be warned: "traditional" winemaking is often synonymous with "poor" winemaking in this region, so opt for more modern producers.

QUALITY The wines of the region tend to be cheap, if not particularly distinguished.

WHITES, REDS AND ROSÉS La Mancha is the largest demarcated wine region in Europe. Shame, then, that its wines aren't better. Lack of water, restrictions on irrigation, old-fashioned technology, cold winters and hot summers mean that La Mancha is not exactly conducive to fine wine production. There are some palatable reds made from Cencibel, but they are hard to find among all those whites made from Airén, grown here because it can withstand almost every harsh condition that La Mancha throws at it.

Valdepeñas, which translates as "Valley of Stones", has a tradition of making light red wines, but these days it makes more whites, again from the ubiquitous Airén. The grape takes up 85 per cent of the vineyards and somehow manages to gate-crash its way into the Cencibel-based rosés and (not bad) red wines of the region.

Utiel-Requena makes pleasant, quaffable reds and rosés from the Bobal and Tempranillo grapes, and these wines are often sold under the name of nearby **Valencia**. **Madrid** produces red and white wines and the region's Tempranillo reds are enjoyable in a simple sort of way.

Southwest of Madrid, **Méntrida** makes robust rosés and strong reds with buckets of tannin mainly from Garnacha and Tempranillo. However, most of the region's wines are fairly ordinary and are sold in bulk for blending.

WINE AND FOOD Drink with caution.

RECOMMENDED PRODUCERS INCLUDE La Mancha: Castillo de Alhambra, El Liso, Piqueras and Torres Filoso.
Valdepeñas: Casa de la Viña, Felix Solís, Los Llanos and Luís Megía.

RECOMMENDED VINTAGES INCLUDE 1990, 1991, 1994, 1995.

TRIVIA Even the most dedicated wine drinkers might be surprised to learn that La Mancha's indigenous white grape, Airén, is (supposedly) the world's most widely planted grape variety.

NORTH–CENTRAL SPAIN

IN A NUTSHELL An exciting mix of old- and new-style winemaking for reds and whites.

GEOGRAPHY Wine regions include Rioja, Navarra, Calatayud, Campo de Borja, Cariñena and Somontano.

WINES, GRAPES AND QUALITY Rioja and Navarra are the stars, and the most notable wines are red. Good Rioja is a pleasure, but rising prices are making it harder to come by.

WHITES AND REDS The **Rioja** DOCa is divided into three zones: Rioja Alta, Rioja Alavesa and Rioja Baja. Rioja's best wines are often a blend of grapes from all three areas. Tempranillo is the main red grape in Rioja, but it is usually blended with smaller amounts of Garnacha, Graciano and Mazuelo (Carignan).

80 per cent of Rioja's production is of red wine. Whites are also made, in the old, oaky style and in a new, crisper style, from Viura, Malvasia Riojana and Garnacha Blanca.

Traditional Riojas spend time maturing in American oak barrels; the label will state how long. *Sin crianza* means the wine has spent no time in oak. For red wines, *crianza* means a wine in its third year consisting of at least one year in oak and the rest in bottle; a *reserva* is aged for a minimum of three years, including one year in oak; and a *gran reserva*, made only in the finest vintages, spends at least two years in oak and three in bottle.

Traditionally **Navarra** made rosé, but the region now produces some good modern reds. Garnacha has long been the main red grape, but Tempranillo and Cabernet Sauvignon are gaining ground as Navarra seeks to emulate, and indeed improve upon, Rioja. There is a trend away from oak-ageing and the reds are usually plummier and fruitier than those of Rioja. The whites, too, are exciting, with lots of Chardonnay being planted. Similarly, **Somontano** is showing promising results and the co-op led **Cariñena** is making its mark.

WINE AND FOOD Soft, mellow, oak-aged Riojas go well with steaks. Navarra reds make good partners for pasta and pizza.

RECOMMENDED PRODUCERS INCLUDE
Cariñena: San Valero.
Navarra: Castillo de Monjardín, Julián Chivite, Guelbenzu, Gurpegui, Ochoa, Palacio de la Vega, Príncipe de Vian and de Sarria.
Rioja: Amézola de la Mora, Barón de Ley, Berberana, Berceo, Bretón, Campillo, Campo Viejo, Contino, Corral, CVNE, Domecq, López de Heredia, La Rioja Alta, Remelluri, Marqués de Cáceres, Marqués de Riscal, Marqués de Villamagna, Martínez Bujanda, Marqués de Murrieta, Marqués del Puerto, Montecillo, Riojanas and Viña Salceda.
Somontano: Alto Aragón (Enate), CoViSa (Viñas del Vero) and Pirineos.

RECOMMENDED VINTAGES INCLUDE 1982, 1983, 1985, 1986, 1988, 1989, 1990, 1991, 1992, 1993, 1994, 1995.

TRIVIA Rioja gets its name from the Rio Oja, a tributary of the River Ebro.

NORTHWEST SPAIN

IN A NUTSHELL This is a region in flux, with new varieties and methods struggling to break free from the restrictions of tradition.

GEOGRAPHY A coastal and inland area that borders Portugal and includes the wine regions of Rías Baixas, Ribeiro, Bierzo, Valdeorras, Cigales and Monterrei.

QUALITY Look for the weighty white wines made from Albariño and the many rosés and light reds of the region.

WINES AND GRAPES A wide range of native grape varieties produce very mixed results.

WHITES, REDS AND ROSÉS The DO of **Rías Baixas** makes much of its wine from hybrid grapes using traditional methods. Albariño is the trendy grape of the moment, and here it makes creamy white wines with beguiling flavours of peach and apricot. These wines are highly sought after by the Spanish and are expensive; the reds of the region, however, are neither sought after, nor expensive.

Ribeiro also makes better whites than reds, with the former accounting for about two-thirds of its production. The Palomino grape has long been used to make most of the white wine, and much of it is boring, but there are moves to make fresher and crisper wines from other grape varieties such as Loureiro, Albariño, Godello, Treixadura and Torrentés. Ribeiro's reds come mainly from Garnacha and various local grapes, but are not greatly exciting.

Valdeorras, the "golden valley", makes red wine from Mencía blended with Garnacha or Cabernet Sauvignon. Much of this wine is sold off in bulk to be blended into generic Spanish wine. Whites are mainly made from the dull Palomino again, although Godello is producing crisp, fresh and aromatic wines that are creating some excitement.

Bierzo and **Cigales** have long been tipped as regions to watch, with juicy reds, attractive rosés and crisp, clean whites hinting at a bright future, but they are taking too long about it. While these regions remain up and coming, others have already arrived.

WINE AND FOOD Albariño whites go well with seafood and paella.

RECOMMENDED PRODUCERS INCLUDE
Bierzo: Palacio de Arganza and Prada a Tope.
Cigales: Frutos Villar.
Rías Baixas: Agro de Bazán, Lagar de Fornelos, Palacio de Fefiñanés, Santiago Ruiz and Vilariño-Cambados.
Ribeiro: Cooperativa Vitivinícola de Ribeiro (Pazo), Lapatena and Viña Mein.
Valdeorras: Senen Guitian Velasco (Viña Guitian).

RECOMMENDED VINTAGES INCLUDE 1987, 1989, 1990, 1992, 1993, 1994, 1995.

TRIVIA Albariño is thought to be a relative of Riesling, brought to northwest Spain by pilgrims travelling to Santiago de Compostela.

IN A NUTSHELL Several fine wines are made here, as well as one stunner – Vega Sicilia, a red wine of jaw-dropping intensity.

GEOGRAPHY This inland region encompasses Ribera del Duero, Rueda and Toro.

WINES, GRAPES AND QUALITY Ribero del Duero produces excellent reds – as good as Rioja – from Tempranillo and Cabernet Sauvignon (among others), while Rueda produces equally fine whites from Sauvignon Blanc, Verdejo and Viura. Toro's reds are mainly Tempranillo-based monsters.

WHITES AND REDS Ribera del Duero is recognised for its superior red wines which, like Rioja, are based on Tempranillo (known here as Tinto Fino or Tinto del País). They are rich, plummy and usually see lots of oak.

The star name of the region (and of Spain) is Vega Sicilia (nothing to do with Sicily), whose reds are made, atypically, from a base of Tempranillo blended with Cabernet Sauvignon, Merlot or Malbec. If Spain had such a thing as a *premier cru*, this would be it. Vega Sicilia is on a par with a Bordeaux first growth, an Italian "Super Tuscan", or Australia's Grange – everyone should try it at least once. Antonio Fernández's Pesquera, made from Tempranillo, is the only other wine that comes close in quality. Sadly, the rest of Ribera del Duero's wines are made largely by co-ops and are maddeningly inconsistent, although quality (and prices) are rising.

Rueda lies northwest of Madrid, near to the city of Valladolid. It used only to produce poor-imitation sherry, but is now making strides with modern white wine, using mainly the aromatic Verdejo grape, often with a dash of Sauvignon Blanc. Verdejo also comes out well with a bit of oak ageing. Other white grapes include Palomino and Viura. A few reds are made from Tempranillo and Cabernet Sauvignon.

Toro is a region to watch, as it hopes to emulate the success of its neighbour, Ribera del Duero. Toro's main grape is Tempranillo (here it is called by yet another name, Tinto de Toro), which is blended with up to 25 per cent Garnacha to produce powerful, rich red wines of high alcohol.

WINE AND FOOD Only drink Vega Sicilia with your favourite food and best friend.

RECOMMENDED PRODUCERS INCLUDE Ribera del Duero: Alión, Felix Callejo, Alejandro Fernández, Pago de Carraovejas, Peñalba-López, Protos, Valduerog and Vega Sicilia.
Rueda: Alvárez y Díaz, Castilla la Vieja and Marqués de Griñon (Durius).
Toro: Fariña and Vega Saúco.

RECOMMENDED VINTAGES INCLUDE 1985, 1987, 1990, 1991, 1994.

TRIVIA Spain has more vineyard acreage than any other country, although it is only the world's third largest wine producer.

SOUTH AND SOUTHEAST SPAIN

IN A NUTSHELL The region is known for its clod-hopping reds and that excellent alternative to sherry, Montilla.

GEOGRAPHY Southeast Spain's main regions are Valencia, Almansa, Yecla, Jumilla, Bullas and Alicante. Southern Spain includes Málaga, Montilla-Moriles and Condado de Huelva.

WINES, GRAPES AND QUALITY Full-bodied reds and crisp, dry whites are made with increasing success in southeast Spain, while the south makes unfashionable but delicious fortified and sweet wines.

WHITES, REDS AND ROSÉS Valencia makes basic white wine from local grape varieties, although foreign investment suggests there is potential for better. Three-quarters of **Almansa**'s production is red, with the Garnacha, Monastrell and Cencibel (Tempranillo again) grapes yielding big reds, although some producers are aiming for lighter styles. In **Condado de Huelva** increasing amounts of ordinary dry table wine are being produced.

Jumilla and **Yecla** have been making strides since *phylloxera* by grubbing up vineyards and replanting with resistant Monastrell clones and foreign grape varieties. The result has been a noticeable improvement (although there is potential for more) in both reds and rosés.

Alicante is the name of both region and grape variety; the grape (otherwise known as Garnacha Tintorera) continues to be grown, although Monastrell is more regularly used for the region's big, dark, alcoholic reds.

SWEET AND FORTIFIED WINES If you like sherry, ignore **Montilla** at your peril. It makes lovely wines that are almost identical to sherry, although they are a little less alcoholic and have slightly less finesse. But good Montilla is better (and a lot cheaper) than poor sherry.

Condado de Huelva makes wines that are similar to sherry, notably Condado *palido* (*fino*-like) and Condado *viejo* (*oloroso*-like), but these are falling from favour.

Málaga has never recovered from being zapped by *phylloxera* in the 1870s, but some producers still make the region's once famous sweet wines, albeit on less than one per cent of the vineyard area of the 19th century.

WINE AND FOOD Montilla goes well with *tapas*; drink sweet wines of Málaga on their own.

RECOMMENDED PRODUCERS INCLUDE
Alicante: Gutiérrez de la Vega.
Almansa: Bodegas Piqueras.
Jumilla: Agapito Rico, Señorío del Condestable.
Montilla-Moriles: Alvear, Gracia Hermanos.
Valencia: Schenk and Vinival.
Yecla: Castaño and Vitivino.

RECOMMENDED VINTAGES INCLUDE Many of these wines are blends of different vintages.

TRIVIA Although *amontillado* means "in the manner of Montilla", Jerez won't let Montilla producers use the term for their own wines.

portugal

NORTHERN PORTUGAL

IN A NUTSHELL Unlike Portugal's most famous export, port, this region's table wines are on the whole tailored for domestic consumption, and are made largely from local grape varieties.

GEOGRAPHY The main regions for growing wine in northern Portugal are the Douro, Bairrada, Dão and Minho.

WINES AND GRAPES Wines range from the big, heavy reds of the Douro to the light, almost fizzy, Vinho Verdes. The region of Bairrada is notorious for producing that icon of our formative drinking years, Mateus Rosé, the bottles of which supported millions of lampshades in the bistros of the 1970s.

There are numerous grape varieties, and local varieties still far outnumber newcomers such as Cabernet Sauvignon, Merlot and Chardonnay. Few wines are sold by the name of the grape, but rather by brand or producer names.

The best-known grapes are Touriga Nacional and Tinta Roriz – famous for their part in making Portugal's greatest gift to the world, port – and the white Alvarinho, which makes the best Vinho Verde and accounts for a quarter of Portugal's wine harvest.

QUALITY Portugal is an old-fashioned country with an old-fashioned wine industry. It suffers from an over-reliance on traditional winemaking and traditional grape varieties. In fact it wasn't until Portugal's entry into the European Union in 1986 that any concession to the outside world was given.

Until then, Portugal had been content to make wine in its own way from its own grapes, confident of a large domestic market. This was not smugness; while being a creditable seventh in the world for amount of wine produced, Portugal is a far more impressive third in the world for per capita consumption.

With EU entry, Portugal realised that to meet the demands of an expectant export market it would have to change its ways and, in many cases, its grape varieties. Yet the local varieties are good and can make excellent wine, and there has been understandable resistance in many quarters to grubbing up traditional varieties just because some foreign consumer would rather have a bottle of Chardonnay.

Denominação de Origêm Controlada (DOC) is the highest quality level for Portuguese wines, followed by *Indicação de Proviniência Regulamentada* (IPR) and then *Vinho Regional*. In many cases, producers who have espoused modern winemaking techniques have had to do so outside the DOC regulations.

WHITES AND REDS Vinho Verde isn't green at all – its name refers instead to the youth of the wines. In fact, most Vinho Verde is red, and little of this is exported (not surprisingly, given that it is usually rather thin and sour). White Vinho Verde, made from Azal Branco, Loureiro, Trajadura and Alvarinho, is infinately better. It should be light and fruity to drink, and usually has an attractive faint sparkle.

The **Douro** is really port country, but several port houses now produce fine table wines. The area is home to the country's top (and most expensive) red table wine, Barca Velha. Made by Ferreira from Tinta Roriz, Touriga Nacional and Tinta Borroca, Barca Velha is produced only in small quantities and only in the best vintages. 18 months in oak gives this full, heavy wine an extra dimension of richness.

Dão is one of Portugal's best regions, producing long-lived red wines with bags of flavour and old-fashioned style from Tinta Roriz (known elsewhere as Tempranillo) and a minimum 20 per cent Touriga Nacional. Plenty of oak ageing ensures that these wines give off great wafts of vanilla. Some quite pleasant, nutty, lemony whites are made here, too.

Big, tannic red wines made from the local Baga grape variety are produced in **Bairrada**; plummy and full-bodied, they spend time in new oak and, although somewhat old-fashioned in style, they are improving noticeably.

WINE AND FOOD Good Vinho Verdes are remarkably refreshing, being faintly sparkling and low in alcohol, and consequently make pleasant *apéritifs* or partners to summer picnics. The red Dãos, Bairradas and Douros need big stews or spit roasts to bring out the best in them.

RECOMMENDED PRODUCERS INCLUDE
Bairrada: Aliança, Quinta das Bágeiras, Casa de Saima, Cava da Insua, Caves São João, Sogrape and Luis Pato.
Dão: Caves São João, Quinta da Cotto, Quinta do Crasto, Grão Vasco, Quinta das Maias, Quinta dos Roques, Quinta de Saes, Santar and Sogrape.
Douro: Quinta da Cismeira, Quinta do Côtto, Quinta do Crasto, Ferreira, Quinta de Gaivosa, Niepoort, Quinta de la Rosa, Ramos-Pinto, Vale do Bomfim and Quinta do Vale da Raposa.
Vinho Verde: Palácio da Brejoeira, Quinta da Aveleda and Solar das Bouças.

RECOMMENDED VINTAGES INCLUDE 1985, 1987, 1988, 1989, 1990, 1991, 1992, 1994, 1995.

TRIVIA Northern Portugal has one of the oldest DOC systems in the world. It was set up in 1756 (180 years before France's) in order to protect the port trade.

SOUTHERN AND CENTRAL PORTUGAL

IN A NUTSHELL This region is home to one of the world's best but least-known fortified wines, Setúbal, as well as to punchy reds.

GEOGRAPHY The main regions for growing wine in southern Portugal are the Alentejo, Bucelas, Ribatejo and Setúbal.

WINES AND GRAPES A mixture of wildly old-fashioned winemaking and state-of-the-art technology produces a wide range of styles. There are fruity red wines made from the local Periquita grape; big, dark reds made from Aragonez (Tempranillo); and plenty of light, crisp white wines.

QUALITY See northern Portugal.

WHITES AND REDS The region of **Terras do Sado**, which covers the whole of the **Setúbal** Peninsula, produces fine reds such as Pasmados and Periquita, both of which are full-bodied wines that need plenty of ageing before they become soft and approachable.

Fruity, easy-drinking red wines come from **Ribatejo**, where local grape varieties combine with Merlot and Cabernet Franc. Near Lisbon, the **Bucelas** DOC yields a fine white wine called Bucellas Velho: a full-bodied, lemony wine which for some reason adds an extra "l" to its name.

In the hot southern region of the **Alentejo**, recent foreign investment has resulted in the addition of stainless-steel tanks and other mod cons, and consequently both the red and white wines are going from strength to strength.

SWEET WINES In **Setúbal**, Moscatel de Setúbal is as good as, and far older than, the similar Muscat de Beaumes-de-Venise. It is grapey, highly alcoholic and utterly delicious.

WINE AND FOOD The whites make good *apéritifs* and partners to light meals; the reds are full and fruity enough to accompany most meat or poultry dishes. Moscatel de Setúbal is smashing when chilled, served on its own or with puddings.

RECOMMENDED PRODUCERS INCLUDE
Alentejo: Herdade de Cartuxa, Herdade do Esporão, Herdade de Mouchão, José de Sousa and Quinta do Carmo.
Bucelas: Caves Velhas and Quinta da Romeira.
Ribatejo: Almeirim, Bright Brothers, Carvalho, Caves Velhas, Fiuza and Quinta da Lagoalva.
Setúbal: JM da Fonseca, Herdade de Cartuxa, Herdade do Esporão, Quinta da Bacalhôa, Quinta do Carmo and JP Vinhos.

RECOMMENDED VINTAGES INCLUDE 1975, 1980, 1983, 1985, 1990, 1992, 1994.

TRIVIA A quirk of the region is the Palace Hotel at Buçaco, which makes greatly sought-after red and white wines that can only be bought at the hotel.

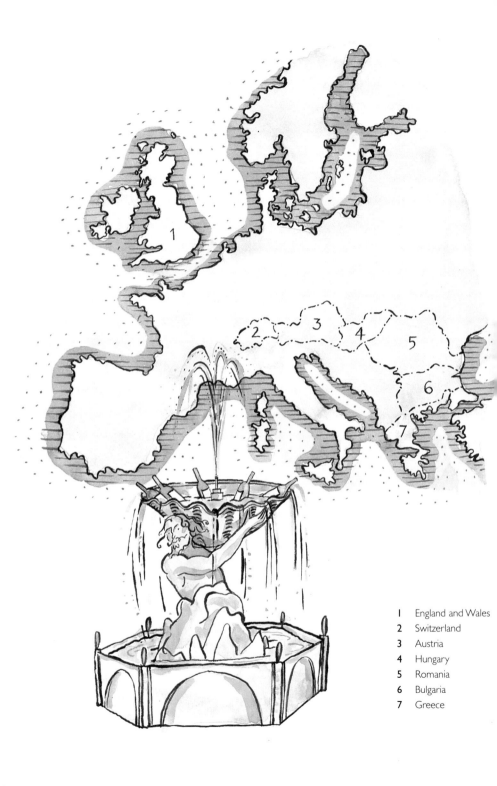

1 England and Wales
2 Switzerland
3 Austria
4 Hungary
5 Romania
6 Bulgaria
7 Greece

rest of europe

AUSTRIA

IN A NUTSHELL 80 per cent of Austrian wine is white, most of which is dry and designed for everyday drinking. Little is exported from this thirsty nation, but the wines most often seen abroad are the stunning dessert wines from the Neusiedlersee in Burgenland.

GEOGRAPHY Wine grapes are grown only in the eastern part of the country. Lower Austria (*Niederösterreich*) contains about three-fifths of the country's vineyards, and the rest are split between Burgenland, Styria and Vienna.

WINES AND GRAPES White wines are made mainly from the Grüner Veltliner, Müller-Thurgau, Grauer Burgunder (Pinot Gris), Welschriesling and Weissburgunder (Pinot Blanc) grapes; a little Chardonnay, Riesling and Sauvignon Blanc is also grown.

Some red wine is made from the Blaufränkisch, Blauer Zweigelt, Blauer Portugieser, Blauburgunder (Pinot Noir), St Laurent and Cabernet Sauvignon grapes.

QUALITY In 1985, Austrian winemaking was shaken to its roots when a few producers were found adding diethylene glycol (better known as antifreeze) to their wines. As it happened, the scoundrels did the industry a favour: the scandal forced an overhaul of regulations and methods, and Austrian wines improved dramatically.

REDS AND WHITES Everyday whites are good, drier and higher in alcohol than those of Germany. Reds are scarce, but worth a try.

SWEET WINES Austrian dessert wines are world-class, and tend to be cheaper and more varied than their French or German equivalents. The foggy conditions of the Neusiedlersee – the huge flat-bottomed lake Austria shares with Hungary – are ideal for botrytis. Look for *ausbruch* wines, which have a raisiny richness.

WINE AND FOOD Dry whites partner cold ham, chicken dishes and freshwater fish; top dessert wines go well with sweet pastries, custard puddings and blue cheeses.

RECOMMENDED PRODUCERS INCLUDE Willi Bründlmayer, Feiler-Artinger, F Hirtzberger, Alois Kracher, Lang, Lenz Moser, Nikolaihof, Willi Opitz, FX Pichler, Josef Pimpel, Franz Prager, Salomon-Undhof, Sattlerh, Servus, Georg Stiegelmar, M Tement, Tschida, Umathum, R Wentzel, F Wieninger, Winkler-Hermaden and Winzer Krems.

RECOMMENDED VINTAGES INCLUDE 1989, 1990, 1991, 1992, 1993, 1994, 1996.

TRIVIA Vienna is the world's only capital city with commercial vineyards within its limits.

BULGARIA

IN A NUTSHELL Bulgaria has long been the most go-ahead of the Eastern European wine countries, and now exports 90 per cent of its wine to an eager market.

GEOGRAPHY The country's soil and climate are ideal for winemaking. New wine laws have divided Bulgaria into five geographical regions: the Danube Valley in the north, the Black Sea region in the east, the Struma Valley in the southwest, and the Maritsa River and Stara Planina in the south.

WINES AND GRAPES Red and white wines are made from international grape varieties as well as from many traditional grapes, such as Pamid, Melnik, Mavrud and Gamza for red, and Dimiat, Misket and Rkatziteli for white. Merlot and Cabernet Sauvignon make the most successful wines, while whites made from Sauvignon Blanc and Chardonnay have yet to do as well.

QUALITY Bulgarian wine is divided into five categories. Quality, the most basic, is hardly "quality" at all; Country Wines are blends of two grape varieties; Reserve and Special Reserve are unblended wines of better quality which are aged for minimum stipulated periods in oak; and wines labelled Controliran (as close to an AC as it gets) are made from specified varieties in controlled areas – this is the label to look for. Although the best Bulgarian reds are Bordeaux-like and have fooled many a connoisseur in blind tastings, the wines still lack the finesse of claret.

WHITES AND REDS Bulgaria makes better wines and exports them more effectively than any of its Eastern European neighbours. In the days before wines from the New World burst onto the scene, the competition consisted mainly of Liebfraumilch, Mateus Rosé and cheap Chianti, compared with which Bulgarian wines, sold under the name of just one grape variety, were a delicious and cheap alternative. But now Bulgarian wines are considered to be old hat when compared with the dazzling whites and reds of Australia, California, Chile and New Zealand. For the moment the UK remains Bulgaria's biggest export market, but there is a danger that Bulgaria's wine exports, already damaged by the dismantling of the former USSR, will be further harmed by changing consumer trends.

WINE AND FOOD Bulgarian reds are highly quaffable and go well with any sort of light meal, from pasta to cold cuts. Whites tend to be rather acidic and should be drunk with food.

RECOMMENDED PRODUCERS INCLUDE Asenovgrad, Damianitza, Haskovo, Khan Krum, Lovico Suhindol, Oriachovitsa, Novi Pazar, Pleven, Rousse, Svishtov and Targovishte.

RECOMMENDED VINTAGES INCLUDE 1990, 1991, 1992, 1993, 1994.

TRIVIA Bulgaria is the world's second largest exporter of wine, after France.

ENGLAND AND WALES

IN A NUTSHELL Formerly regarded as a harmless hobby for gentle eccentrics, winemaking in England and Wales is now a serious and successful business, the results of which are a pleasure to drink.

GEOGRAPHY There are about 1000 hectares (2,500 acres) under vine, with 400 or so wineries scattered through Suffolk, Essex, Kent, Sussex, Surrey, Berkshire, Hampshire, Somerset, Hereford and Wales.

WINES AND GRAPES Although one or two producers flirt with Pinot Noir, most English wines are white, made chiefly from German-style grape varieties and hybrids such as Huxelrebe, Müller-Thurgau, Seyval Blanc, Reichensteiner, Bacchus, Schönburger, Kerner, Madeleine Angevine and Ortega. Recent plantings include Chasselas, Pinot Blanc, Sauvignon Blanc and Chardonnay.

QUALITY Let's get one thing straight: English wine is *not* British wine. English wine is subject to strict controls, made from grapes grown and vinified in Britain (Welsh wines are obliged to be labelled as English too). British wine is an unspeakable slush made from imported grape juice.

English wines are well worth sampling as the industry comes of age and the wines begin to develop a distinctive style. Look for wines marked with the English Vineyard Association (EVA) seal (now known as the United Kingdom Vineyard Association). Sadly, the best English wines can be pricey.

WHITE, ROSÉ, SPARKLING AND SWEET WINES English white wine ranges in style from Germanic-medium to Loire-dry, and should be light, fresh, crisp, flowery and zippy. Some producers are experimenting with oak-ageing, while others are making exciting sparkling wine – after all, southern England shares with Champagne chalky soil, a cool climate and grapes that are high in acidity. Some good rosés and, surprisingly, luscious late-harvest dessert wines, are also being made.

REDS Pinot Noir is the most successful red grape, but few reds are made.

WINE AND FOOD English wines are light and delicately flavoured and can be overwhelmed by rich foods, so keep matches simple. Well chilled, they make refreshing *apéritifs*, and few things are more pleasing than English wine with good old fish and chips.

RECOMMENDED PRODUCERS INCLUDE Adgestone, Astley, Barkham Manor, Breaky Bottom, Bruisyard St Peter, Chapel Down, Chiddingstone, Denbies, Hidden Springs, Lamberhurst, Northbrook Springs, Nyetimber, Sharpham, Staple St James, Tenterden, Thames Valley Vineyards, Three Choirs, Wootton and Wyken.

RECOMMENDED VINTAGES INCLUDE 1989, 1990, 1994, 1995, 1996.

TRIVIA Two million bottles of English wine are produced every year.

GREECE

IN A NUTSHELL Having made wine since time began, Greece sadly disproves the adage that practice makes perfect. But, luckily, there is more to life than Retsina and now, at last, an exciting renaissance is taking place.

GEOGRAPHY The wine-growing areas are most simply divided into four: northern Greece (which includes Macedonia and Thrace), central Greece (comprising Epirus, Thessaly and Attica), the Peloponnese and the Greek Islands.

WINES AND GRAPES Foreigners might be forgiven for thinking that the only thing Greece produces is that epitome of acquired taste, Retsina. In fact, stylish wines of real quality are being made at last, both from indigenous grape varieties (hard to spell and even harder to pronounce) and the better-known international ones.

QUALITY It is true that dull, flabby wines that are high in alcohol and often oxidised can still be found. But, thanks to the introduction of a strict appellation system and the almost single-handed efforts of winemaker John Carras, more and more stylish wine can be found. However, this welcome renaissance is not helped in Greece itself by the fact that, all too frequently, shops and restaurants spoil the wines by storing them poorly. Abroad, potential consumers are put off Greek wines by their frequently unpronounceable names and high prices.

WHITES Retsina is the national wine. Chiefly from **Attica**, it is made from Saviatiano which is mixed with tiny amounts of pine resin. Some impressive whites are now being made and include wines from international varieties such as Chardonnay and Viognier.

REDS Agiorgitiko is the country's main red grape, grown largely in the **Peloponnese**. In **Macedonia** and **Thrace** the most important grape is the red Xynomavro, which is good for blending or making single varietals. The wines tend to be deeply flavoured and are surprisingly elegant.

SWEET WINES Greece's sweet wines can be marvellous, whether they be the white ones made from Muscat or the port-like reds made from Mavrodaphne.

WINE AND FOOD Greek wine slips down most easily when accompanied by a plate of fried calamari, hummus or taramasalata. They are also ideal for cross-cultural cuisine.

RECOMMENDED PRODUCERS INCLUDE Antonopoulos, Boutari, Calliga, Domaine Carras, Gaia, Gentilini, Hatzimichalis, Kourtakis, Château Lazaridis, Château Matsa, Papaioannou, Strofilia and Tsantali.

RECOMMENDED VINTAGES INCLUDE 1990, 1993, 1995.

TRIVIA The biggest export market for Greek wines is Germany.

HUNGARY

IN A NUTSHELL Tokaji (also known as Tokay) is the star of the show – it is one of the world's greatest dessert wines.

GEOGRAPHY The main wine regions are the Great Plain in south central Hungary (which makes over half of the total production), Lake Balaton, Mátraalja, Eger and Tokáji.

WINES AND GRAPES In addition to Tokaji, the country produces wine from several unpronounceable local grape varieties as well as from more classic ones.

QUALITY As a rule Hungary's wines are competently made but undistinguished, Tokaji being the obvious exception.

WHITES Full-bodied dry white wines are made from Furmint, with lighter and fresher ones coming from Olaszrizling (Welschriesling). Chardonnay provides plenty of cheap wines that are attractively crisp and lively, as does, increasingly, Sauvignon Blanc.

REDS Light red wines are made from Pinot Noir and fuller ones from Merlot and Cabernet Sauvignon. Bikavér, or Bull's Blood, used to be Hungary's best-known table wine, but these days it is disappointing.

SWEET WINES Produced in northeast Hungary, **Tokaji** is made from Furmint blended with Hárslevelu. Botrytis-affected grapes (known as *aszú*) are picked separately from unaffected ones, which are made into a

rough, dry base wine called *szamorodni*. The botrytis-affected grapes are fermented and made into a paste, which is measured in tubs known as *puttonyos* before being added to the *szamorodni* for a further fermentation. How sweet the final wine is depends on how many *puttonyos* of *aszú* are added: three *puttonyos* makes a medium-dry wine and six a very sweet one. Sweeter still is Tokaji Aszú Essencia, made only in exceptional years from hand-picked grapes.

Sweetest of all is Tokaji Essencia, made from the juice of grapes crushed only by their own weight. The juice is fermented for years in oak barrels, although in practice this wine is so sweet that it hardly ferments. It is outrageously delicious and savagely expensive; but given that one of its alleged properties is its ability to bring one back from the dead, the price might be considered fair.

WINE AND FOOD The reds and whites are conventional enough to go with most foods. Tokaji is almost a pudding in itself.

RECOMMENDED PRODUCERS INCLUDE Danubiana, European Wine Producers Group, Gyöngyös, Hungarovin, Neszmély and Royal Tokaji Wine Company.

RECOMMENDED VINTAGES INCLUDE 1988, 1990, 1993, 1994, 1995.

TRIVIA Tokaji was the first wine ever to have been deliberately made from grapes affected by botrytis.

ROMANIA

IN A NUTSHELL Romania makes good, cheap, everyday wines, but old-fashioned techniques and too many years spent supplying the former USSR have hindered progress.

GEOGRAPHY The best regions are Dealul Mare in the Carpathian foothills, Tîrnave in the northeast of the country, Murfatlar near the Black Sea and Cotnari in the north, which makes fine sweet wines.

WINES AND GRAPES Three-quarters of the wines are white. Feteasca Alba and Welschriesling are the most planted white grape varieties, but others include Feteasca Regala, Frîncusa, Tamaîiosa, Gewürztraminer, Muscat, Riesling, Pinot Gris, Grasa and Chardonnay. Red grapes include Cabernet Sauvignon, Babeasca, Feteasca Negra, Merlot and Pinot Noir. Vintages are not of much consequence for many of these wines.

QUALITY To the surprise of many, Romania is one of the world's top 10 wine-producing countries and the sixth-largest wine grower in Europe, yet it exports only 15 per cent of its production. The potential for making quality wines has been wasted by years of supplying the former USSR with cheap, sweet wines. As a result, Romania's wine industry lags far behind that of Bulgaria.

WHITES, REDS AND SWEETS Much Romanian wine is dull and flabby, but newly equipped wineries are beginning to produce cleaner, fresher examples. They are greatly aided by

the many international grape varieties that are growing alongside indigenous ones. As a rule the whites are better than the reds, although Pinot Noir, Cabernet Sauvignon and Merlot are good. The native red grape variety Feteasca Neagra makes an earthy, liquorice-flavoured wine, if you like that sort of thing.

Tîrnave in northern Romania is the most highly regarded region, with **Moldavia** making the best sweet wines.

Cotnari, a region in the northeast, produces a rich, sweet, botrytised wine made from the Grasa, Feteasca Alba and Tamaîoasa grape varieties, called, unsurprisingly, Cotnari. This is Romania's finest wine – it used to be as famous as Hungary's Tokaji. Cotnari tastes like honeycomb and almonds and comes from the only vineyard still planted exclusively with Romanian varieties.

In the southeast, **Dealul Mare** produces the best Cabernet Sauvignons and Pinot Noirs, although **Murfatlar** near the Black Sea also makes good examples of both.

WINE AND FOOD Good quaffing wines, they go well with light meals and friendly gatherings.

RECOMMENDED PRODUCERS INCLUDE Paulis, Pietroasa, Prahova and Rovit.

TRIVIA The inhabitants of Oltenia have a curious saying: "When you drink a glass of Riesling from Dealul Viilor, the penknife starts out alone in your pocket." Mmm, must try it some time…

SWITZERLAND

IN A NUTSHELL Switzerland is one of the world's top 20 wine producers, but little wine is exported, partly because the Swiss drink more than they can make.

GEOGRAPHY Like the country itself, the wine regions are divided roughly between the French, Italian and German cantons. The French-speaking cantons include the main vineyard areas of Vaud and Valais, the most productive German-speaking cantons are Zürich and Schaffhausen, while the most notable Italian-speaking canton is Ticino.

WINES AND GRAPES Fendant (also known as Chasselas, Dorin, Gutedel and Perlan) is the most widely planted white grape, producing low-acid, low-alcohol, though racy and full-bodied, white wines. Red wines are made mainly from Pinot Noir and Gamay, often blended together into a wine called Dôle. In the Italian areas, the most popular grape is Merlot. Other grapes grown include Riesling, Barbera, Pinot Gris (Malvoisie de Valais), Pinot Blanc and Müller-Thurgau.

QUALITY The wines are expensive, idiosyncratic in style and largely white.

WHITES AND REDS The largest wine-producing canton is **Valais** in western Switzerland. It is home to around 20,000 small growers and the dominant wines are red, mainly made from Pinot Noir and Gamay.

Four-fifths of the vineyards in **Vaud** are planted with Fendant, which produces white wines that range from the bland to those with Loire-like steeliness.

East Switzerland includes all of the 16 German-speaking cantons. Pinot Noir (known here as Blauburgunder) is the most important grape variety, followed by Müller-Thurgau, Pinot Gris and Gewürztraminer. 70 per cent of the wine is red.

Merlot dominates in the **Ticino** region (southern Switzerland), making soft, velvety reds and the pale, pink Merlot Bianco. The best Merlots made here carry the *Viti* seal, for which they have been tasted and assessed.

WINE AND FOOD Dôle and Fendant go well with fondues, poultry and hard cheese, and Fendants are also ideal with salmon or seafood.

RECOMMENDED PRODUCERS INCLUDE Henri Badoux, Louis Bovard, Caves Imesch, Cave de la Côte-Uvavins, Domaine E de Montmollin Fils, Les Frères Dubois & Fils, Robert Gilliard, Luc Massy Vins, Mauler, Les Perrières, Provins Valais, Hans Schlatter, Tamborini Carlo, Valsangiacomo 1831, Frédéric Varone Vins, Vins des Chevaliers and Weinbau & Kellerei.

RECOMMENDED VINTAGES INCLUDE 1993, 1994, 1995, 1996.

TRIVIA The Swiss drink four times as much wine per head as the British and their per capita consumption is higher than that of Spain or Greece.

OTHER MEDITERRANEAN COUNTRIES

Cyprus

To its shame, Cyprus continues to produce grape juice concentrate for making into "British" wine. In a country which really should be making decent wines, the only producers of note are ETKO, KEO and SODAP, who all create some drinkable reds.

The most highly favoured grape is Mavron, which not only makes earthy red table wines, but is also blended with Xynistyeri to make the country's one wine of importance: a potentially luscious and intense dessert wine called Commandaria.

Lebanon

Unquestionably, Lebanon's finest wine is Château Musar, whose vineyards are situated on Mount Barouk, overlooking the Bekaa Valley. Armed troops among the vines are reportedly a fairly common sight.

Owned by the single-minded and Bordeaux-trained Serge Hochar, Château Musar was set up in the 1930s by his father. The property regularly produces excellent wines of warmth and elusive, savoury sweetness, from a blend of Syrah, Cabernet Sauvignon and Cinsault. Less impressive white wines are made from Chardonnay, Sauvignon Blanc and Muscat.

The other main producer is Château Kefraya. Its Rouge de Kefraya is a blend of Cinsault and Carignan, while Château de Kefraya mixes Cabernet Sauvignon with small amounts of Mourvèdre, Syrah and Grenache. Both wines, unlike Musar's, are designed for drinking young.

united states and canada

CALIFORNIA

IN A NUTSHELL A vibrant, exciting area where an ideal climate, massive investment, modern technology and American innovation are resulting in some world-class wines.

GEOGRAPHY The state of California is on the west coast of the United States. The main vineyard areas are the Central Coast (Carmel Valley, Livermore, Salinas Valley/Monterey, San Luis Obispo, Santa Barbara, Santa Cruz Mountains); South Coast (Temecula); North Coast (Los Carneros, Mendocino, Lake Napa, Sonoma); and the Interior (Amador, Lodi, San Joaquin Valley, Sierra Foothills).

WINES AND GRAPES Chardonnay is the main white grape, from which big, buttery wines are made for an insatiable domestic market. Cabernet Sauvignon is Chardonnay's red equivalent, yielding blockbusting single varietals and co-producing many Bordeaux or Rhône-style blends. California's "own" grape, Zinfandel, makes wonderful, spicy, full-bodied reds and the soda-pop rosé known as "white Zinfandel".

There are also sizeable plantings of Chenin Blanc, Sauvignon Blanc, Riesling, Gewürztraminer, Pinot Blanc, Muscat, Sémillon, Grenache, Carignan, Pinot Noir, Merlot, Gamay and Syrah. The relentless search for the perfect wine sees other varieties come and go: current favourites include Barbera, Mourvèdre and Viognier.

So closely has California copied France that for a long time California wines were labelled simply as "Burgundy", "Claret" or "Champagne". Although some growers continue this practice, most top producers now prefer to label their wines by the name of the grape varieties they contain, making the wines much more accessible to consumers.

California single varietals can be less pure than those from other countries, as regulations insist that wines labelled as single varietals need only contain 75 per cent of the named variety. Many such wines might more correctly be labelled as blends.

Recently, winemakers have begun to produce so-called "Meritage" wines: blends that mirror even more closely the wines of Bordeaux by using Cabernet Sauvignon, Merlot and Cabernet Franc, or the wines of the Rhône by using Syrah, Grenache and Mourvèdre. The name "Meritage" came about after a competition was held to choose a term to describe such wines; it sounds suitably (but not off-puttingly) French, while coyly suggesting a marriage of grape varieties. Tuscany is another classic Old World region that is now being used as a role model by Californians.

One aspect of California that is alien to many European winemakers is that each winery produces a number of different wines. Go to Château Margaux in Bordeaux, for example, and all you will see is its excellent blended claret. Go to Beringer in California and you'll find between 25 and 30 types of red, white, blended, single varietal, fortified and dessert wines produced from 13 different grape varieties.

QUALITY Despite the setback of a recent bout of *phylloxera*, California goes from strength to strength. It produces 95 per cent of all US wine and is the world's sixth-largest wine producer.

California does have an appellation system for its wine-producing areas, known as Approved Viticultural Areas (or AVAs), but the system is far less comprehensive than any in Europe. It is solely geographical, containing no restrictions as to permitted grape varieties or methods of production.

A bottle's label will give the name of the state and the region or the county from which the wine comes. At least 85 per cent of the grapes must be from the specified area; the remaining 15 per cent may come from anywhere else in California. Indeed, the winery itself might not even be in the AVA that appears on the label, since many wineries own or buy grapes from vineyards in neighbouring areas. Until such time as the AVAs begin to reflect the characteristics of certain grapes grown in different areas, the producer's name will remain all-important.

As one might expect, cutting-edge technology is used in the pursuit of excellence in California; Robert Mondavi, for example, is experimenting with satellite imaging to detect the warmest sites for new vineyards. It is this kind of attitude that makes for exciting winemaking and wines.

SPARKLING AND SINGLE VARIETAL WHITES
California wines are generally good value. Ignore the mass-produced jug wines and head straight for the excellent *méthode traditionelle* sparkling wines, which are tastier (and cheaper) than many champagnes.

Chardonnay is believed by many Californians to be the only grape capable of making white wine, and examples in the past have tended to be big, fat monsters full of oaky flavours. Fortunately, some producers have learned to tone them down.

SINGLE VARIETAL REDS A fine Zinfandel can be a spicy, spirited treat of a red wine, and a good 100 per cent Cabernet Sauvignon or Cabernet-based blend will show the variety at its most exuberant.

BLENDED WINES California blends can be as exciting as the state's single varietals. To pick a random example, Beringer's 1996 Alluvium Blanc is described as 60 per cent Sémillon, 26 per cent Sauvignon Blanc, 10 per cent Chardonnay and four per cent Viognier, and exhibits a fascinating combination of flavours.

The beauty of California is that if such a blend doesn't work, winemakers can try

something different next year. New blends are always coming onto the market, so as a consumer it is important to identify a producer you like and keep abreast of what's on offer. In France, strict appellation laws make this sort of experimentation impossible, but in California producers are gloriously uninhibited and are bound neither by tradition nor legislation.

FORTIFIED AND SWEET WINES California's dessert wines can be bewitching, and are made not just from Sémillon and Sauvignon, as might be expected, but from more obscure varieties such as Orange Muscat, Black Muscat and the Sémillon-Gewürztraminer cross known as Flora. Some surprisingly good fortified wines are produced too, including some made, improbably enough, from Cabernet Sauvignon.

WINE AND FOOD The biggest and best Zinfandels, Cabernets and blended red wines need roast meats or hearty casseroles. Regular Sauvignons and Chardonnays go well with plain fish or chicken, whereas the full-flavoured, oaky examples can stand heavily-sauced dishes.

RECOMMENDED PRODUCERS INCLUDE
Napa Valley: Acacia, Beringer, Caymus, Clos du Val, Corison, Cuvaison, Diamond Creek, Dominus, Duckhorn, Flora Springs, Frog's Leap, Grgich Hills, Heitz, Louis Martini, Robert Mondavi, Mumm Napa Valley, Newton, Opus One, Joseph Phelps,

St Clement, Schramsberg, Silverado, Spottswoode, Stag's Leap, Trefethen and Chateau Woltner.
Rest of California: Arrowood, Bonny Doon, Byron Vineyards, Clos du Bois, Carneros Creek, Ferrari-Carano, Fetzer, Firestone, Foxen, Gallo, Glen Ellen, Gloria Ferrer, Gundlach-Bundschu, Iron Horse, Jordan, Matanzas Creek, Nalle, Quady, Quivira, Qupé, Ridge, Roederer Estate and Wild Horse.

RECOMMENDED VINTAGES On the whole, California vintages are consistent in terms of quality, although there are occasional variations. The date on the label is often more useful as an indication of the wine's maturity than of the vintage's quality.

TRIVIA Wine from the region is known as California wine, rather than Californian wine. Presumably the Californians know why.

PACIFIC NORTHWEST

IN A NUTSHELL It is said with increasing conviction that the best Pinot Noir grown outside Burgundy comes from Oregon, and that for pure intensity of flavour, the wines of Washington are hard to beat. Idaho has yet to become a major player.

GEOGRAPHY The region known as the Pacific Northwest comprises the three US states of Idaho, Oregon and Washington.

WINES AND GRAPES Whites, including Chardonnay, Sémillon, Gewürztraminer, Riesling and Pinot Gris are successful. Pinot Noir from Oregon and Merlot from Washington continue to dazzle.

QUALITY The appellation system is similar to that of California.

WHITES AND REDS The success of **Oregon** is due to that most capricious of grapes, Pinot Noir, which grows particularly well in the Willamette Valley AVA. Riesling, once the most popular variety here, continues to make excellent late-harvest wines, but is now taking a back seat not only to Pinot Noir, but also to Chardonnay and Pinot Gris. Gewürztraminer, Müller-Thurgau, Sémillon and Zinfandel are also being planted more frequently.

Winemaking started in **Washington** in the 1870s, but international varieties weren't planted here until the 1900s. Since the mid-1960s the wine industry has blossomed, and Washington is now the second-largest producer of high-quality wine in the US (after California). Most vineyards are in the east of the state, where the Cascade Mountains block the cool, damp weather that rolls in from the west. Varied microclimates mean that different grapes thrive in different areas, although on the whole Merlot is stunningly successful and Cabernet Sauvignon, Sauvignon Blanc, Sémillon, Chenin Blanc and native varieties such as Concord also flourish.

WINE AND FOOD Oregon Pinot Noir is as good with roast pork as it is with grilled salmon. Try Washington Cabernet Sauvignons and Merlots with casseroles.

RECOMMENDED PRODUCERS INCLUDE Oregon: Adelsheim Vineyard, Amity, Argyle, Bethel Heights, Cameron, Chehalem, Cooper Mountain, Domaine Drouhin, Edgefield, Elk Cove, Erath, The Eyrie Vineyards, Henry Estate, Firesteed, Ken Wright Cellars, Laurel Ridge, Panther Creek, Ponzi, Rex Hill, Sokol Blosser, Tualatin and Yamhill Valley.
Washington: Andrew Will, Barnard Griffin, Château Ste-Michelle, Chinook, Columbia Crest, DeLille Cellars, Hedges, The Hogue, Kiona, L'Ecole No 41, Leonetti, Quilceda Creek, Salishan, Seven Hills, Snoqualmie, Stewart, Woodward Canyon and Yakima River.

RECOMMENDED VINTAGES INCLUDE 1985, 1987, 1988, 1992, 1993.

TRIVIA Washington is on the same latitude as Bordeaux.

NEW YORK

IN A NUTSHELL The planting of popular international grape varieties in place of unappealing local hybrids is showing the world New York's potential.

GEOGRAPHY Northeastern state between the Atlantic and the Great Lakes.

WINES AND GRAPES Most of the grapes are blended into generic wines from no specified region. However, some decent reds and whites are made. Extensive new plantings of Cabernet Sauvignon, Chardonnay, Pinot Noir and Riesling (mostly in the Hamptons) have taken place, but international grape varieties still account for less than six per cent of the vineyards. Local grapes such as Catawba, Concord, Delaware and Niagara comprise 80 per cent, and hybrids such as Aurora, Baco Noir, Chelois, De Chaunac and Seyval Blanc make up the rest. Riesling and Chardonnay have been the most successful of the newly planted grape varieties.

QUALITY Most New York vineyards are planted with local or hybrid grapes which are not good enough to make decent wine. Consequently the state has not, until recently, been regarded as a producer of quality wines. Nevertheless, there are over 100 wineries in New York, with many of the best wines being made in small wineries, known as "farm wineries". But with competition from California, which is more used to growing the classic international varieties, New York's wines will have to be very good to be taken seriously.

WHITES AND REDS The three most productive areas are the Finger Lakes, the Hudson River region and Long Island. The latter's two viticultural areas of North Fork and the Hamptons both have potential.

Finger Lakes yields good German-style white wines and decent Chardonnay. The Gulf Stream gives **Long Island** a Bordeaux-like microclimate, which fosters good Riesling and Chardonnay; the latter's more austere flavours are closer to Chablis than California.

A lot of New York's production goes into generic wines labelled "Burgundy", "Chablis", "Rhine Wine" and "Sauternes". When a wine is designated AVA, it must contain at least 85 per cent of that area's wine; wines labelled "New York State" must contain at least 75 per cent of the state's wine.

WINE AND FOOD The wines are good value, so quaff them liberally. The Chardonnays go particularly well with fish and poultry.

RECOMMENDED PRODUCERS INCLUDE Benmarl, Bridgehampton, Canandaigua Wine Co, Clinton Vineyards, Cascade Mountain, Eaton, Fox Run, Glenora, Gristina, Hargrave, Heron Hill, Lamoreaux Landing, Lenz, Millbrook, Palmer, Pellegrini, Pindar Vineyards, Royal Kedem, Standing Stone, Swedish Hill, Wagner, Walker Valley, Hermann J Wiemer and Woodbury.

RECOMMENDED VINTAGES INCLUDE 1993, 1994, 1995, 1996.

CANADA

IN A NUTSHELL Small amounts of decent wine are being made in the climatically challenged Canada, but they are not widely seen abroad.

GEOGRAPHY Vines are grown mainly in the provinces of Ontario in the east of the country and British Columbia in the west.

VINES AND GRAPES Most of the grapes used are hardy hybrids that can survive Canada's freezing winters: De Chaunac, Marechal Foch, Seyval Blanc and Vidal Blanc, or American varieties such as Catawba, Concord, Elvira and Niagara.

However, producers are planting international varieties including Gamay, Chardonnay, Gewürztraminer, Pinot Noir and Riesling, as well as tiny amounts of Pinot Blanc, Pinot Gris, Pinot Meunier, Chenin Blanc and Auxerrois, all of which will make better wine if they can overcome the weather. Riesling and Chardonnay are faring especially well among white wines; the country's reds are still fairly basic.

Canada's best wines are its Icewines, made from the juice pressed from frozen grapes, usually Riesling and the hybrid Vidal. Try them.

QUALITY A regulatory organisation called the Vintners' Quality Alliance was set up in Ontario in 1988 and in British Columbia in 1990 to oversee the winemaking industry. Its strict regulations for permitted grapes and vineyard specifications have done a lot to improve and promote Canada's wines.

WHITES AND REDS Canada makes wine in four provinces: British Columbia, Nova Scotia, Ontario and Quebec. The country doesn't make much wine, however, and consumes five times what it produces.

Canada's climate is too limiting to enable the country to be a consistent producer of decent wine, but two states in particular are making drinkable stuff: **Southern Ontario**, which makes 85 per cent of the country's Designated Viticultural Area (DVA) wine in Pelee Island, Lake Erie North Shore, North Shore and the Niagara Peninsula; and **British Columbia**, which makes the rest in the DVAs of Okanagan Valley, the Similkameen Valley, the Fraser Valley and Vancouver Island, where the lakes temper the climate, making it similar to that of eastern Washington.

WINE AND FOOD Concentrate on the white wines and drink them with seafood. The Icewines are delicious on their own.

RECOMMENDED PRODUCERS INCLUDE Blue Mountain, Cave Spring, Château des Charmes, Gray Monk, Henry of Pelham, Hillebrand Estates, Inniskillin, Lang Vineyards, Mission Hill, Quails' Gate, Sumac Ridge, Vincor International and Vineland Estates.

RECOMMENDED VINTAGES INCLUDE 1993, 1994, 1995, 1996, 1997.

TRIVIA Canada is the world's largest producer of Icewine.

south america

ARGENTINA

IN A NUTSHELL Although Argentina's wine is rapidly improving, most is still cheap and ordinary, aimed at the apparently unquenchable domestic market.

GEOGRAPHY 70 per cent of Argentina's vineyards are planted in Mendoza, the other main regions being Río Negro, Neuquén, San Juan, La Rioja (not to be confused with Rioja in Spain), Salta, Jujuy and Catamarca.

WINES AND GRAPES Most wines are red, the best being made from Malbec or Criolla (also known as Mission). However, experiments with classic red varieties, particularly Cabernet Sauvignon, are proving successful. White grapes such as Palomino, Torrontes and Pedro Ximénez are used for Argentina's plentiful fortified wines, while Chardonnay, Sauvignon Blanc, Chenin Blanc, Riesling, Sémillon, Torrontes, Viognier and Pinot Gris are used for dry whites.

QUALITY Argentinian wine has in the past been compared unfavourably with Chilean wine. While Chile forged ahead with massive investment, modern technology and international grape varieties, Argentina's 2,000 wineries bumbled along producing poorly made, old-fashioned wine from obscure local grapes. Yet conditions are good – dry air means few diseases and there is no *phylloxera*.

The red wines are the most interesting, whether made from the many Italian or the more recently introduced French grapes. Malbec is capable of producing the best wines in Argentina. There is a lack of good producers, but exceptions include Weinert, whose Carrascal (Malbec/Cabernet/Merlot) is delicious, and Trapiche.

The future looks bright. There are plenty of new plantings, and several important foreign producers such as Mumm, Deutz, Piper-Heidsieck and Moët et Chandon have invested.

WINE AND FOOD Reds go well with roast meats and barbecues, while whites should be kept in the refrigerator... permanently.

RECOMMENDED PRODUCERS INCLUDE La Agrícola, Arizu, Balbi, Bianchi, Catena, Esmeralda, Etchart, Navarro Correas, Norton, Peñaflor, El Recreo, San Telmo, Santa Ana, Pascual Toso, Trapiche, Viña Patagonia and Weinert.

RECOMMENDED VINTAGES INCLUDE 1993, 1994.

TRIVIA Argentina is the fifth largest wine-producer in the world.

CHILE

IN A NUTSHELL Chile makes some very good wine indeed, but as yet no great wine. Its vineyards have the advantage of never having been afflicted with *phylloxera*.

GEOGRAPHY Most vineyards lie in the country's long Central Valley area, and are concentrated in two main areas: around the capital, Santiago, and around Curicó. There are also vineyards further south around Maule.

WINES AND GRAPES Most of the grapes grown in Chile today are of French origin, winemakers from France having brought over cuttings of their traditional varieties in the 1850s. Remarkably enough, the red Pais grape still takes up about half the country's vineyards, even though little of its wine is exported. Chile's wines are almost always sold under the name of their grape varieties.

QUALITY Chile has the ideal conditions for growing grapes. The regions are dry and situated neatly between deserts, mountains and seas, with cooling breezes that combat any excessive heat. Rain never threatens the harvest, but vineyards are kept watered by melting snows from the Andes. *Phylloxera* never got a foothold in Chile's sandy soil, so the vines (many of which are very old) are the original rootstock. Yet Chile has a problem: because conditions are so easy for winemakers, there is no incentive to be experimental and innovative. This might seem harsh, because some terrific wines are

being made, but too much Chilean wine is still indifferent. The country offers some of the best value around, and there are some exceptional wineries, but many producers rely on a buoyant export market without trying as hard as they might.

The lifting of the government ban on planting new vineyards in 1974 has helped to revitalise the industry. Producers including Château Lafite-Rothschild (which owns half of Los Vascos), Bruno Prats (of Château Cos d'Estournel), Paul Pontallier (of Château Margaux), Franciscan Vineyards and Miguel Torres, have invested money and know-how in the country, which will raise standards further. Torres, who is credited with introducing stainless steel to the industry, expressed great belief in Chile, calling it a "viticultural paradise".

With European expertise hand-in-hand with Chile's natural advantages, there is every chance that in a few years time, Chilean wine will be as good as, say, that of California.

WHITE AND SWEET WINES The better white wines are less successful than the red, but they are still fresh, clean and well-made. Sauvignon Blanc is making headway; new clones have been planted and it is yielding light, grassy wines, especially in the **Casablanca Valley** – a region which is also producing good Chardonnay. Zesty, fresh white wines come from the **Curicó** and **Maule** valleys.

Sémillon makes dry wines and, more recently, some interesting late-harvest ones.

A few very good wines from Riesling and Gewürztraminer have also been produced.

REDS Merlot and Cabernet Sauvignon are the most successful grape varieties in the country, making soft, balanced, juicy and flavourful wines. It is said that they don't age well – but who cares? Although they may lack the intricacy of fine clarets, they are juicily typical of their varieties.

Regions whose wines are worth looking out for include the **Aconcagua Valley**, which is home to excellent rich, blackcurranty Cabernets. In the large **Central Valley** area, the **Maipo Valley** is best for juicily delicious Cabernets, as is the **Rapel Valley**, which also produces intense Pinot Noirs and plummy Merlots.

One oddity is Carmenère, which also goes under the name of Grand Vidure. Hardly anyone has heard of it and its wines rarely leave Chile, but it has a Merlot-like plumminess.

WINE AND FOOD Treat the reds as you would any claret from Bordeaux, and drink them with roast meats, homemade hamburgers or cheese and biscuits. The Sauvignon Blancs are great partners for seafood.

RECOMMENDED PRODUCERS INCLUDE Agrícola Aquitania, Balduzzi, Bisquertt, Caliterra, José Cánepa, Carmen, Carta Vieja, Casa Lapostolle, Casablanca, Concha y Toro, Cousiño Macul, Echeverría, Errázuriz, Gracia, Luís Felipé Edwards, Miguel Torres, Montes, Mont Gras, San Pedro, Santa Carolina, Santa Rita, Torreón de Paredes, Undurraga, Los Vascos and Villard.

RECOMMENDED VINTAGES INCLUDE Chilean vintages are consistent and the wines are designed for drinking young.

TRIVIA Vineyards were first established in Chile during the 16th century by the Spanish, who planted large amounts of the red variety, Pais.

OTHER LATIN AMERICAN COUNTRIES

Brazil

Most of Brazil's wine is for domestic consumption or for export to the United States. Humid vineyards in sub-tropical conditions are not ideal places in which to grow grapes, but productivity is amazingly high, with as many as five crops being harvested every two years.

Many grapes are undistinguished, but recent plantings include Barbera, Cabernet Sauvignon, Chardonnay, Merlot, Nebbiolo, Pinot Blanc, Riesling, Sémillon, Seyval Blanc and Trebbiano. Brazil's wines could be described as dire but, given that august companies such as Moët et Chandon, Domecq, Cinzano and Martini & Rossi have detected enough potential to invest in the industry, this may be too harsh.

Mexico

The country proudly boasts America's oldest wine industry, which dates back to 1521, but there is little else for it to crow about as far as wine is concerned. Most of Mexico's crop is distilled into brandy or used as table grapes or raisins, and the locals quite sensibly prefer to drink beer.

The most drinkable wines come from Baja California, where grapes such as Cabernet Sauvignon, Nebbiolo and Petite Sirah are grown. However, as with Brazil, recent foreign investment from the likes of Domecq, Martell and Freixenet, suggest that improvements may well be on the way.

Peru

Tacama Vineyards in Ica Province produce drinkable Cabernet Sauvignons, Sauvignon Blancs and sparkling wines. A growing export market is encouraging producers to address the problems of *phylloxera* and oxidisation that have hitherto plagued the industry.

Uruguay

A thirsty home market and a desire to increase the country's meagre exports have encouraged Uruguayan winemakers to revamp the industry. Five quality wine regions were set up in 1992.

The leading grape variety, Tannat, which accounts for a third of all plantings and makes hefty reds and rosés, is making way for more accessible varieties such as Cabernet Sauvignon, Merlot, Chardonnay, Sauvignon Blanc and Viognier.

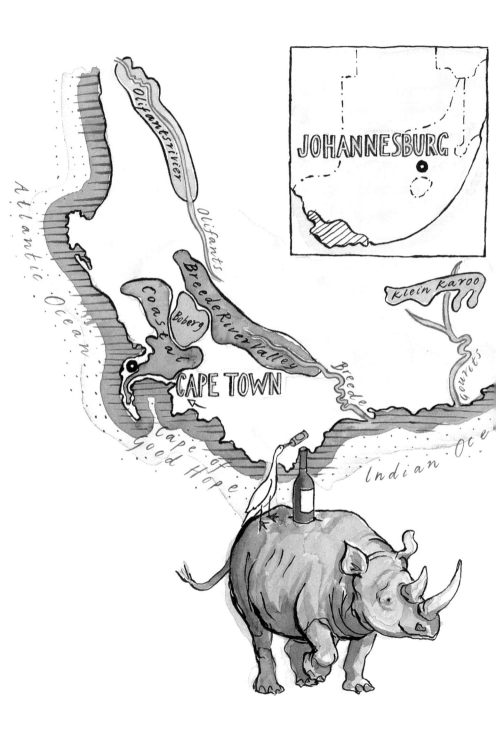

africa

SOUTH AFRICA

IN A NUTSHELL South Africa is the seventh-largest wine producer in the world, and its wines are improving each year.

GEOGRAPHY The main wine-growing areas are all in the southwest of the country.

WINES AND GRAPES Sauvignon Blanc and Chenin Blanc (known locally as Steen) are great successes. The red Pinotage is an acquired taste; it says "burnt rubber" to many European palates, but the South Africans seem to like it. The most-planted international red grape is Cabernet Sauvignon, but pockets of Merlot and Shiraz also exist.

QUALITY In the early 1900s, the problems of over-production were confronted by the formation of the cooperative wine growers' association, the KWV (Kooperatiewe Wijnbouwers Vereniging van Zuid-Africa), whose brief was to control the supply and demand of grapes and ensure consistent pricing. In 1972 a system of quality control known as Wine of Origin (similar to the AC system of France) was established, which divided South Africa's wine-producing areas into 13 wine districts. To complicate matters, some of these districts overlap regions.

Although South Africa makes good wines, they could and should be better. The country has never reached the heights of California, Australia or New Zealand. Its strength lies in the production of good, cheap supermarket wines, almost all of which are white, light, crisp, fresh and fruity, but not very exciting.

The **Cape** area, with its perfect climate and diverse soils, produces most of the country's wines. Its production was dominated by "port" and "sherry" from 1900 to the 1970s, when medium-dry to semi-sweet white table wines in the German fashion became popular.

The Boberg region includes the districts of **Paarl** and **Tulbagh** (both of these are also covered by the Coastal region). The Coastal region is home to the districts of **Durbanville, Stellenbosch, Constantia** and **Swartland**. The inland Breede River Valley region encompasses the districts of **Robertson, Swellendam, Tulbagh** again and **Worcester**.

The main wine districts are Paarl and Stellenbosch. **Paarl** has extensive wineries and research stations and is warmer and drier than Stellenbosch. Paarl is home to many top-quality growers and co-operatives, and is the centre of the "sherry" and "port" industry.

Stellenbosch has excellent and varied growing conditions, with many microclimates, and is home to the largest number of well-known producers, including Meerlust, Rust-en-Vrede and Blaauwklippen.

WHITE AND SPARKLING WINES Wines are labelled varietally. The most popular white is Steen, followed by Chardonnay, Cape Riesling (Crouchen), Clairette Blanche, Colombard, Green Cape (Sémillon), Hanepoot (Muscat), Palomino, Riesling and Sauvignon Blanc.

Sauvignon Blanc is thriving, and is possibly happier here than in California, Australia or Chile. Chardonnay has great potential and Steen will continue to be popular. The *méthode traditionelle* sparkling wines known as Cap Classique aren't quite as successful as they could be, but they are getting better all the time.

REDS Much less red is made than white, and the whites are finer. However, Cabernet Sauvignon and Merlot show signs of doing well, although neither is widely planted yet. Cinsaut (called Hermitage), Shiraz and Pinotage are the most successful red grapes so far, but Cabernet Franc and Pinot Noir are also commonly seen. The top red wines tend to spend too much time in wood and the grapes are often not ripe enough when picked.

Pinotage was created by a crossing Cinsaut with Pinot Noir. It produces big, burly, chewy wines, not unlike Shiraz, but without the latter's style, as Pinotage is far too one-dimensional. As wines from Cabernet Sauvignon and Shiraz begin to impress consumers, surely Pinotage will fall away. There cannot be that big a market for liquid burnt rubber outside South Africa... well, you try it.

FORTIFIED AND SWEET WINES To the annoyance of the Portuguese, South Africa's "ports" are very good. They are made from the same grapes as port proper, and are well worth trying. Riesling is best in dessert wines.

WINE AND FOOD The whites are good with fish and seafood dishes and on their own; the reds go well with barbies, roasts and grills.

RECOMMENDED PRODUCERS INCLUDE Backsberg, Bellingham, Blaauwklippen, Le Bonheur, Boschendal, Buitenverwachting, De Westhof, Delheim, Dieu Donné, Fairview Estate, Graham Beck, Groot Constantia, Hamilton Russell, Hartenberg, Jordan, Kanonkop, Klein Constantia, KWV, Long Mountain, Meerlust, Montpellier, Mulderbosch, Nederburg, Rustenberg, Rust-en-Vrede, Saxenburg, Simonsig, Simonsvlei, Spier, Steenberg, Stellenbosch, Thelema, Twee Jongegezellen, Vergelegen, Villiera, Vriesenhof, Warwick and Welgemeend.

RECOMMENDED VINTAGES INCLUDE 1986, 1989, 1991, 1992, 1993, 1994, 1995, 1996.

TRIVIA Over half of South Africa's production goes to distillation or for grape juice concentrate (of which South Africa is the world's largest producer).

Algeria

North Africa has a wine-growing tradition that stretches back to the Romans, but quality is not good. Algeria once produced vast quantities of quite decent wine, much of which was exported to France for blending, and often (whisper it if you dare) for adding backbone to wines of world acclaim.

However, since independence the amount of wine produced in Algeria has fallen dramatically, as has its quality. Nowadays, most grapes are used as table grapes rather than for wine production, not least because of the Muslim disapproval of alcohol.

Winemaking techniques remain resolutely old-fashioned, with big, beefy, rather "cooked" wines being made from Alicante Bouschet, Cabernet Sauvignon, Carignan, Cinsault, Clairette, Grenache, Mourvèdre, Syrah and Ugni Blanc.

Morocco

Morocco uses the same grape varieties as Algeria to make acceptable Bordeaux and Rhône-style reds and Grenache-based rosés. The wines tend to be full-flavoured and almost sweet, with high levels of alcohol. As with Algeria, quality deteriorated after independence from France, and the region has yet to rediscover its form.

Tunisia

Tunisia makes some decent reds and rosés around the Gulf of Tunis, which are rarely seen abroad, as well as some surprisingly fine Muscats, which are either dry or headily sweet.

Zimbabwe

Some wines are produced in Zimbabwe, but most are of little interest. The country suffers from severe rain at harvest time and poor quality grapes, and there are only two producers of any repute – Mukuyu and Stapleford.

1 Barossa Valley
2 Mudgee
3 Hunter Valley
4 Upper Hunter Valley
5 Yarra Valley

1 Auckland
2 Gisborne
3 Hawke's Bay
4 Marlborough
5 Canterbury

australia and new zealand

NEW SOUTH WALES AND VICTORIA

IN A NUTSHELL The Hunter Valley in NSW is one of Australia's most important wine regions. Victoria is famous for its dessert wines.

GEOGRAPHY Vineyard areas are widely spread throughout the two regions.

WINES AND GRAPES Top grapes in NSW are Shiraz, Semillon (no é) and Chardonnay. Stars in Victoria are sparkling Shiraz and Liqueur Muscat.

QUALITY Just 20 years ago the only Australian wines readily available abroad were Kanga Rouge and Wallaby White, both known for containing a hangover in every bottle. How things have changed! Far from being laughed at by winemakers in France, Italy and Spain, Australian producers are now being copied and even asked – no, begged – for their advice.

WHITES AND REDS New South Wales (NSW) is second only to South Australia as the centre of Australia's wine industry. The best region is the **Hunter Valley**. Rosemount has helped put NSW on the map with its Chardonnay, Semillon and Shiraz wines, which often spend time in oak. These boisterous beauties are as far from shrinking violets as you can get. Pinot Noir and Cabernet Sauvignon are also grown in NSW, and look out for good Chardonnay and Merlot from **Mudgee**.

Northeast Victoria makes several types of wine, including sparkling Shiraz. There is delicious sticky dessert wine, including Liqueur Muscat and Tokay from Rutherglen, good Cabernet, Shiraz and Liqueur Muscat from Glenrowan and, in Milawa, Brown Bros makes everything from dry whites to dessert wines.

Central Victoria has good, big reds and sparkling wines. **South Victoria** offers good red Bordeaux-style blends and fine Pinot Noir, Chardonnay and sweet wines, while the **Yarra Valley** yields elegant Rieslings and Chardonnays.

FOOD AND DRINK Big whites need heavily sauced foods. Shiraz is fab with steak.

RECOMMENDED PRODUCERS INCLUDE
NSW: Botobolar, Brokenwood, Evans Family, Huntington Estate, Lindemans, McWilliam's, Tulloch, Tyrrell's, Rosemount and Rothbury.
Victoria: Balgownie, Bannockburn, Bass Phillip, Best's, Brown Bros, Coldstream Hills, Craiglee, Chambers, Dalwhinnie, De Bortoli, Giaconda, Jasper Hill, Merrick's, Mitchelton, Morris, Stoniers, Seppelt, Chateau Tahbilk, Taltarni, Tarrawarra, Yarra Yering, Yeringberg, Yellowglen.

RECOMMENDED VINTAGES INCLUDE
NSW: 1985, 1986, 1987, 1991, 1992, 1993, 1994, 1995.
Victoria: 1985, 1986, 1988, 1990, 1991, 1992, 1993, 1994, 1996.

SOUTH AUSTRALIA

IN A NUTSHELL South Australia is one of the world's most successful wine-producing regions. It is best-known for the blockbusting reds from the Barossa Valley and Coonawarra.

GEOGRAPHY The central southern state of Australia includes the main wine regions of the Barossa Valley, Eden Valley, Adelaide Hills, Coonawarra, Padthaway, Clare, McLaren Vale, Langhorne Creek, Kingston and Riverland.

WINES AND GRAPES The main red grapes are Cabernet Sauvignon, Grenache, Malbec, Merlot, Mourvèdre, Shiraz and Pinot Noir. White grapes include Chardonnay, Riesling (known as Rhine Riesling), Semillon and Sauvignon Blanc.

The greatest successes are the Barossa's massive, full-throated Shiraz and Coonawarra's pole-axing Cabernet Sauvignons, but there are also top-class whites – especially Riesling – and excellent botrytis-affected sweet wines.

QUALITY For a country of Australia's size, little wine is made, but South Australia is top dog in the production stakes in terms of quantity and quality. It produces two-thirds of the annual harvest and makes bulk wine as well as some of the country's biggest, richest reds and best cool-climate whites.

WHITE, RED, SPARKLING AND SWEET WINES
The **Barossa Valley** is the biggest quality wine-producing district in Australia, and almost every Australian wine company is represented there. The first plantings were undertaken by German Lutherans in the 1840s, largely to make "ports", "sherries" and dessert wines, but nowadays the region is celebrated for the excellence of its sumptuous, opaque Shiraz and its richly textured blended wines.

Coonawarra is Barossa's big rival. Good Chardonnays, Sauvignons and Rieslings are made here, but Coonawarra is most famous for its red wines. Shiraz used to be the most planted grape variety, and it is still used to make rip-roaring wines, but Cabernet Sauvignon has edged ahead in popularity, producing wines of striking complexity which are stuffed full of blackcurrant and mint flavours.

However, the finest wine in all Australia, and indeed one of the finest in the world, is Penfolds Grange Hermitage, which, since 1994, has simply been called Grange. Originally made entirely from old-vine Shiraz (it now usually has a small dollop of Cabernet Sauvignon in it, too), Grange is a wine of staggering intensity with a formidable concentration of fruit.

South Australia's other regions seem pale beside the bravura displays of Barossa and Coonawarra, but there are good wines to be had. **Padthaway** makes similar Chardonnays to those produced in Coonawarra and is making a mark with its sparkling wines. Its reds are OK, but not as good as the whites. The **Clare Valley** produces decent Semillon, Chardonnay and Shiraz wines, but its

Rieslings are considered to be best of all. The **Southern Vales** region is best for blended wines, although the sub-region of **McLaren Vale** is acclaimed for its Shiraz, Cabernets, Sauvignons and Chardonnays, which are almost as flamboyant as those from Barossa and Coonawarra. **Langhorne Creek** is up-and-coming, with its vines situated on vast flood plains, and **Kingston** in the southeast is a new-comer that is building a solid reputation. Stunning reds are also made in the **Eden Valley**, where Henschke's Hill of Grace Shiraz is talked about in almost the same hushed tones as Penfolds Grange. Top Chardonnays and Sauvignon Blancs can also be found in the **Adelaide Hills**.

WINE AND FOOD The reds of South Australia are big indeed, and often the best way to drink them is with barbies, stews, game or even simply with Cheddar.

RECOMMENDED PRODUCERS INCLUDE
Adelaide Hills: Croser/Petaluma, Lenswood, Nepenthe, Penfolds, Petaluma Shaw and Smith and Stafford Ridge.
Barossa: Basedow, Wolf Blass, Grant Burge, Leo Buring, Elderton, BRL Hardy, Krondorf, Peter Lehmann, Charles Melton, Penfolds, Rockford, St Hallett, Seppelt and Yalumba.
Clare: Jim Barry, Grosset, Knappstein, Leasingham, Tim Adams and Wendouree.
Coonawarra: Brands, Hollick, Katnook Estate, Leconfield, Lindemans, Mildara, Orlando, Petaluma, Penley Estate, Rouge Homme, Rymil, Wynns and Zema.
Eden Valley: Heggies, Henchke and Mountadam.
Langhorne Creek: Bleasdale, Lake Breeze.
McLaren Vale: Coriole, Chapel Hill, Chateau Reynella, d'Arenberg, Hardy's, Geoff Merrill, Seaview and Wirra Wirra.

RECOMMENDED VINTAGES INCLUDE 1982, 1984, 1985, 1986, 1987, 1988, 1990, 1991 1993, 1994, 1996.

TRIVIA From being a beer-loving nation, Australia now consumes about 20 litres of wine per head per year.

WESTERN AUSTRALIA

IN A NUTSHELL Western Australia produces vibrantly fruity Chardonnay, Semillon, Sauvignon Blanc, Shiraz and Pinot Noir.

GEOGRAPHY Climate is the limiting factor in all these regions, which can either be too hot or too cold and dangerously short of rain.

WINES, GRAPES AND QUALITY Western Australia's wines are often Bordeaux-like in style, with great depth of flavour. Tasmania is beginning to make some head-turning fizz.

WHITES AND REDS Western Australia is bakingly hot in the **Swan Valley**, which has tended to make big, burly wines. Its great success has been "Houghton's White Burgundy" (more usually called "HWB"), made from Chenin Blanc, Muscadelle and, more recently, Chardonnay. It is consistently Australia's best-selling white wine.

The slightly cooler areas of the **Margaret River** and lower **Great Southern Regions** produce rich and intense red wines of great concentration, mainly from Shiraz, Cabernet Sauvignon (excellent in Margaret River), Pinot Noir, Merlot and some Zinfandel. Classy white wines are also made from Chardonnay, Sauvignon, Riesling and Semillon.

Tasmania is too cool for Cabernet, but Chardonnay, Riesling and sometimes Pinot Noir can be lively and delicate. **Queensland**'s main wine-growing area is Stanhope/Roma, which makes some half-decent Shiraz and successful Chardonnay/Semillon blends.

The **Northern Territory** is hot but, amazingly, Alice Springs of all places is home to the celebrated Chateau Hornsby which, through sheer bloody-mindedness and ingenuity, produces drinkable reds and whites.

SPARKLING WINES Some good sparkling Pinot Noir/Chardonnays are made in **Tasmania** and, given time, they should get better.

WINE AND FOOD Western Australian whites are full enough to tackle spicy food, and the reds are great with stews or cassoulets. Try the Tasmanian sparklers with oysters, and drink Chateau Hornsby with, well, astonishment.

RECOMMENDED PRODUCERS INCLUDE
Canberra: Doonkuna and Lark Hill.
Great Southern (WA): Goundrey, Plantagenet and Wignalls.
Margaret River (WA): Amberley, Ashbrook, Brookland Valley, Cape Mentelle, Cullen, Devil's Lair, Evans and Tate, Leeuwin Estate, Moss Wood, Pierro and Vasse Felix.
Northern Territory: Chateau Hornsby.
Queensland: Robinsons Family Vineyard.
Swan Valley (WA): Capel Vale, Paul Conti, Houghton and Sandalford.
Tasmania: Freycinet, Heemskerk, Moorilla Estate, Piper's Brook and Rochecombe.

RECOMMENDED VINTAGES INCLUDE 1985, 1986, 1987, 1988, 1990, 1991, 1992, 1994, 1996.

NEW ZEALAND

IN A NUTSHELL In the space of barely 20 years, New Zealand has gone from producing no Sauvignon Blanc to producing some of the best in the world.

GEOGRAPHY Most of New Zealand's vineyards lie in coastal areas that are warmed by the sun during the day and cooled by sea breezes at night. Being close to the International Date Line, the grapes are the most easterly in the world and consequently the first to see the sun each day.

The North Island's main regions are Auckland, Gisborne/Poverty Bay, Hawke's Bay, Waikato and the Bay of Plenty, and Wairarapa/Martinborough; the South Island's are Marlborough, Canterbury, Nelson, and Central Otago.

WINES AND GRAPES Hybrid grapes have been grown in New Zealand since the 1820s, but it wasn't until the 1960s that producers started to experiment with European varieties. Conditions were always seen to favour the production of white wine, and Müller-Thurgau was deemed to be the perfect grape. Consequently, this variety was widely planted and proceeded to produce well-made but intensely dull imitations of Liebfraumilch. Thank goodness, then, for Montana which, in 1973, planted an experimental batch of Sauvignon Blanc in the corner of one of its vineyards. It was an instant success.

New Zealand Sauvignon Blancs are simply wonderful, packed with gooseberry and asparagus flavours and crisp acidity. The

Chardonnays, too, are excellent. The country's reds aren't quite as accomplished, but Cabernet Sauvignons and Merlots are soft and juicy, and Pinot Noir does well.

All of the country's wines are sold under the name of the grape varieties they contain. They are not cheap and they do not always compare well in price terms with similar wines from Australia, Chile, South Africa or even France. But they are a joy to drink and nobody with the slightest interest in wine should ignore them.

QUALITY An old joke has an airline pilot telling his passengers that they would soon be landing at Blenheim Airport: "Please fasten your seat belts and extinguish your cigarettes," he says, "and for those of you wishing to change your watches to local time, set them back 20 years." Yet New Zealand has had the last laugh, because it is now a world leader in the wine stakes – especially in the production of Sauvignon Blanc which, it can be argued, no other country or region does better.

WHITES When New Zealanders set their minds to do something, they tend to do it well. So, on discovering that they had been sold a pup with Müller-Thurgau, wine producers were determined to make up for lost time by making their Sauvignon Blanc the best in the world.

On the market for barely two decades, New Zealand Sauvignons are already regarded by many as the tops (though funnily enough not in the Loire). The wines bring out all the grape's characteristics, such as its grassy, nettle-like, cat's pee aroma, which you either love or hate.

Compared with Sancerres and Pouilly-Fumés, New Zealand's Sauvignons might appear to be too much of a good thing, with their almost overwhelming gooseberry flavours, but to many they are unbeatable. The wines rarely spend time in oak – producers believing that consumers should taste wine, not wood.

Thankfully, Müller-Thurgau is now largely ignored as New Zealand plays to its strengths. But Sauvignon is not the only game in town, and wines of dramatic quality are being made from other classic varieties. The best Sauvignons come from **Marlborough**, as do rich, heady Chardonnays.

Gisborne makes lovely creamy Chardonnays and distinctive Gewürztraminers, while producers in **Hawke's Bay**, **Auckland** and **Canterbury** are succeeding with crisp, stylish Rieslings.

REDS Hawke's Bay and **Auckland** make some vivid Merlots and Cabernet Sauvignons, while Pinot Noir does best in cooler **Martinborough** and the South Island's **Central Otago**.

SPARKLING AND SWEET WINES Fine dessert wines made from botrytised Riesling and excellent sparkling wines come from **Marlborough**.

WINE AND FOOD The thrillingly fresh flavours of New Zealand's white wines cry out for equally fresh seafood and fish, plucked straight from the deep rather than the deep-freeze. Reds are a good partner for barbecues, kebabs and plain meat dishes.

RECOMMENDED PRODUCERS INCLUDE
North Island: Ata Rangi, Babich, Brookfields, Clearview, Collards, Cooks, Corbans, Delegat's, Dry River, Esk Valley, Goldwater, McDonald Winery, Matua Valley, Millton, Montana, Morton Estate, Ngatarawa, Palliser, Sacred Hill, Selaks, Stonyridge, Te Mata, Te Motu, Vidal and Villa Maria.
South Island: Cloudy Bay, Domaine Chandon, Giesen Estate, Highfield, Hunters, Jackson Estate, Lawson's Dry Hills, Montana, Nautilus, Vavasour, Waipara Springs, Wairau River and Wither Hills.

RECOMMENDED VINTAGES INCLUDE 1985, 1986, 1987, 1989, 1990, 1991, 1996.

TRIVIA New Zealand may be a small country, but its elongated shape means that if it were transposed to Europe, it would stretch from the Rhine Valley in the north, through Alsace, Champagne, Burgundy, the Loire and Bordeaux into southern Spain.

madeira, port & sherry

MADEIRA

IN A NUTSHELL George IV called Madeira "the best wine in the world", but these fortified wines have long since fallen out of favour, despite their flavours and longevity.

GEOGRAPHY Madeira comes only from the Portuguese island of Madeira in the Atlantic, some 640 kilometres (roughly 400 miles) west of Morocco.

WINES AND GRAPES During the 18th century, Madeira was used on ships as ballast and to prevent scurvy. Two crossings of the equator, with soaring temperatures in the hold, mellowed the acidic wines wonderfully.

Nowadays, the fermented wine is effectively "cooked" (*estufagem*): the vats of wine are kept in hot stores (*estufas*), where temperatures reach 45°C (120°F). The wines are fortified up to 18 per cent and are matured in a *solera* system, similar to that used for sherry.

Four main grape varieties are used, each lending its name to the style of wine: Sercial, Verdelho, Bual and Malmsey. The wine must contain at least 85 per cent of the named variety.

QUALITY Madeiras have an amazing ability to age, even for 200 years. Once opened, they remain in good condition almost indefinitely.

STYLES *Sercial* is the driest of all Madeiras and makes an excellent *apéritif*.
Verdelho is soft, medium-dry, and again makes an ideal *apéritif*.
Bual is dark, fruity and full-bodied.
Malmsey is the sweetest – dark and fragrant, with a luscious honeyed taste, great before bed.

Madeira labels generally feature one of the following: *Reserve* (five years old); *Special Reserve* (at least 10 years old); *Exceptional Reserve* (at least 15 years old); *Vintage*: (single variety and vintage and are at least 22 years old).

WINE AND FOOD Soups (dry styles), biscuits or walnuts (medium styles), and sweet tarts or even blue cheeses (sweetest styles).

RECOMMENDED PRODUCERS INCLUDE Blandy, HM Borges, Cossart Gordon, Henriques and Henriques, The Madeira Wine Company, Miles and Pereira d'Oliveira.

RECOMMENDED VINTAGES INCLUDE 1908, 1910, 1931, 1950, 1954, 1957, 1961, 1966, 1969, 1971.

TRIVIA Much of Madeira's flavour comes from the island's unique potash soil. Legend has it that Captain João Gonçalves, sent to claim Madeira for Portugal in the 1400s, started a fire, destroying the island's forests and changing the soil forever.

PORT

IN A NUTSHELL Australia, South Africa and California may make port-style wines, but they do not make *port*! This most famous fortified wine comes only from Portugal.

GEOGRAPHY The vineyards which produce port are situated along the River Douro in northern Portugal.

WINES AND GRAPES The original port wine zone was given its limits in 1756. Up to 18 grape varieties are permitted in the blended wine, the most prominent of which is Touriga Nacional. Grape spirit is added to the wine before fermentation ends, the unfermented sugars accounting for the wine's sweetness.

The town of Oporto, from whence the wine takes its name, is situated in the mouth of the Douro River. It is to Oporto that the newly blended wines are brought – often on old-fashioned and picturesque sailing barges – prior to export, having aged in the lodges which surround the town of Vila Nova de Gaia.

QUALITY Price can be a guide, from cheap rubies to dearer vintages.

STYLES There are many types of port, but broadly speaking they fall into three categories: ports that are matured in wood, ports that are matured in bottle, and ports that like it both ways.

Wood port is blended from the wines of several different years and is aged in wooden casks, maturing more quickly than its vintage

counterparts. Wood port leaves its sediment in the cask and, once bottled, will mature no further, being ready to drink immediately without the need for decanting.

Ruby port is so-called because of its bright colour. It is the most basic example of its type, made from lower quality grapes. The wines are aged in wood for two years before being bottled while they are still vibrant, full of fruit and very sweet.

Tawny port also takes its name from its colour. It is blended from several different years and spends much longer in wooden casks than ruby port (anything from 10 to 40 years). It is lighter and nuttier in flavour than vintage port and doesn't need to be decanted. Its label will state how long the wine has been aged; a 40-year-old tawny being something special. These wines are excellent served chilled.

Vintage port is made only in exceptional years, and only from the best grapes, harvested from the finest sites. It spends two years in wood before being bottled without filtering, after which it matures in the bottle, taking at least 10 to 15 years before it is ready to be drunk. By then, it will have a large sediment and will need decanting. Port producers decide by consensus whether or not a particular harvest is good enough to warrant "declaring" it a vintage year. If the vintage is not good enough, the wines will be used to make other styles of port. So, unlike wines such as burgundy or claret, which are made in good years and bad, vintage port is only occasionally produced.

Single quinta port – a port house might decide to produce a vintage port from one of its high-quality estates in a year that is not officially declared. Such ports are known as single quinta ports (a *quinta* being a vineyard or a wine estate). Although they don't always enjoy the prestige (or command the high prices) of a full-blown vintage, single quinta ports are more often than not just as good. Taylor's Quinta de Vargellas is a striking example. Indeed, so successful have such wines been that, confusingly, some companies declare them in *bona fide* vintage years, too.

White port is made in the same way as other ports, but using white grapes. It is often drunk with ice or tonic and can be sweet or dry.

Crusted port is beneath vintage port and old tawnies in terms of quality, and is blended from the wines of different years. It is aged in wood for three to four years, completing its maturation in bottle, which causes it to throw a sediment or "crust".

Late bottled vintage port (LBV) is the level of quality below crusted port. It is wine from a single year that is not quite the quality of vintage, and is kept in cask for twice as long as a vintage port – between four and six years – and is filtered before bottling. The result is lighter in colour and flavour than vintage port and ready to drink earlier. Its label will state both the date of its vintage and its bottling.

Vintage character port is a blend of high-, but not top-, quality wines from several vintages, aged in cask for about five years before being filtered and bottled, by which time it is ready to drink.

WINE AND FOOD An old Portuguese proverb states that "all wine would be port if it could". This may be overstating the case, but a fine port in its prime is unbeatable. White port makes a very good *apéritif* when chilled, an old tawny is perfect with biscuits, cake or rich puddings, and a long-lived vintage is ideal with Stilton and other strong cheeses.

RECOMMENDED PRODUCERS INCLUDE Churchill, Cockburn, Croft, Delaforce, Dow, Ferreira, Fonseca, Gould Campbell, Graham, Offley, Quinta de la Rosa, Quinta do Noval, Sandeman, Smith Woodhouse, Taylor and Warre.

RECOMMENDED VINTAGES INCLUDE 1955, 1960, 1963, 1966, 1970, 1975, 1977, 1980, 1983, 1985, 1992, 1994, 1997.

TRIVIA Asked to recommend a good port, a well-known wine merchant (who shall remain nameless), having just returned from a long and arduous wine tasting, replied: "Ever tried Folkestone?"

SHERRY

IN A NUTSHELL Sherry is one of the world's finest wines and, although imitations exist, true sherry can only come from one designated area in southern Spain.

GEOGRAPHY Sherry comes from the deep southwest corner of Spain, centred round the towns of Jerez de la Frontera – from where it gets its name – and Sanlúcar de Barrameda.

WINES AND GRAPES British merchants arrived in force in Spain in the 1800s, establishing large sherry houses such as Sandeman and Duff Gordon. Many of these still exist.

Sherry is a fortified wine made from the Moscatel, Palomino and Pedro Ximénez grapes. The fermented wines are divided into categories, depending on their ageing potential, and the sherries are aged in a *solera* system, blending young and old wines to ensure freshness and consistency of style. Sherry generally does not have a vintage date.

QUALITY Ignore so-called Cyprus, British or South African sherry (except for cooking with or for making Bloody Marys). Spanish sherry has a unique flavour drawn from the scuzzy film of yeast called *flor* that grows on the wine's surface.

STYLES *Fino* is dry, delicate and tangy; its zip and freshness make it a great *apéritif* – drink it young, chilled, and within a week of opening. *Manzanilla* is the lightest, driest and saltiest;

this is a *fino* made not in Jerez but in neighbouring Sanlúcar, where wind from the sea is said to impart a salty tang to the wine and it is the best appetite kick-starter. *Fino-amontillado* is a fino which has lost its *flor* and is turning into an *oloroso* style. *Amontillado* is a *fino* which has been aged, giving it a darker colour and a nuttier, chewier flavour. Usually dry in Spain, it is often made medium-dry for export. Best served at room temperature.
Pale Cream is a sweetened *fino*.
Palo Cortado is a cross between a *fino* and an *oloroso*.
Oloroso is packed with concentrated fruit aromas; *olorosos* are usually dry in Spain, but can be sweetened for export.
Pedro Ximénez is a rarely seen, intensely sweet, black-coloured sherry. An interesting after-dinner drink or conversation piece.

WINE AND FOOD Dry sherry is a good *apéritif*, and goes with soup, potted shrimps, tapas, avocado vinaigrette, *crudités*, pâté, ham, *hors d'oeuvres* and chicken livers. Sweeter sherries are good with mince pies.

RECOMMENDED PRODUCERS INCLUDE Barbadillo, Croft, Domecq, Garvey, González Byass, Harveys, Hidalgo, Lustau, Osborne, Sandeman and Valdespino.

TRIVIA Sherry plays an important part in the Scotch whisky industry, with distilleries buying and importing old sherry barrels from Jerez in which to age their whisky.

red grapes

CABERNET SAUVIGNON

(Synonyms: Petit-Cabernet, Vidure, Sauvignon Rouge)

MAINLY GROWN IN Australia, Bordeaux, Bulgaria, California, Chile and Italy.

ALSO GROWN IN Greece, Lebanon, New Zealand, Portugal, South Africa and Spain.

STYLE A deep purple-red colour. The aroma has flashes of blackcurrants, raspberries, mint, cherries, tobacco and eucalyptus. The juicy, jammy, complex flavours, with structure and tannin, give the wines great ageing potential.

VINES Cabernet Sauvignon is the most successful, popular and sought-after red grape in the world. As the primary grape of Graves and the Médoc in Bordeaux it makes stunning clarets. In California it is the basis of most of the state's top red wines. It is also becoming popular in Spain, where it is often blended with Tempranillo. Lighter wines are made in New Zealand and South Africa.

AUSTRALIA Blackcurrant flavours are foremost. Lean, clean and fruity on its own, Cabernet Sauvignon is usually blended with Shiraz to produce full, plummy, concentrated wines. Coonawarra is the country's most highly favoured spot for Cabernet.

BORDEAUX Cabernet Sauvignon is *the* grape of Bordeaux, although single varietals are rarely made. The grape is blended with

Cabernet Franc, Malbec, Merlot or Petit Verdot to produce claret, and its aptitude for ageing is enhanced by lengthy maturation in oak. Elsewhere in France, quality Cabernets are also made in Bergerac and Buzet in the southwest, and in the Loire and Languedoc.

BULGARIA Excellent single varietals and blends are produced here, particularly in the Suhindol region. While not terribly exciting when compared with wines from California or Australia, these are nonetheless good value.

CALIFORNIA The best examples usually come from Napa and Sonoma. Here Cabernet Sauvignon was traditionally a single varietal grape, although tiny amounts of Merlot and Cabernet Franc now creep in to make "Meritage" wines. Much of the blackcurrant flavour is touched with eucalyptus and mint, and the "Meritage" wines tend to be fuller and sweeter than their claret counterparts.

CHILE Deliciously inky wines, with great intensity of fruit.

ITALY Cabernet Sauvignon is grown in Piemonte and Emilia-Romagna. It is also used to great effect in the non-DOC "Super Tuscans". Typically, it has crisp acidity levels and less mouth-puckering tannin than are found elsewhere.

GRENACHE

(Synonyms: Cannonau, Garnacha Tinta, Garnacho Tinto, Grenache Noir)

MAINLY GROWN IN France (particularly Languedoc-Roussillon and the southern Rhône) and Spain.

ALSO GROWN IN Algeria, Australia, California, Corsica, Israel, Morocco and Sardinia.

STYLE Grenache is particularly suited to hot, windy vineyards. It produces quite pale wine that is high in alcohol, with hints of sweetness, ripe raspberry fruit and an underlying pepperiness.

WINES The world's second most widely planted red grape, Grenache is the primary variety of the southern Rhône's Châteauneuf-du-Pape. It is designed for blending, but can produce pleasant Beaujolais-style wines made by carbonic maceration. Its low tannin and fruit flavours also make it ideal for rosé.

FRANCE Here Grenache is mainly grown in the southern half of the Rhône Valley, where it is usually blended with Cinsault, Carignan, Syrah and Mourvèdre. It provides up to 80 per cent of the blend of Châteauneuf-du-Pape, the remaining 20 per cent being divided between 12 other varieties. Also in the southern Rhône, Grenache is the dominant grape in the big, boisterous wines of Gigondas and is transformed into much of region's rosé, most notably Tavel, Lirac, Côtes du Rhône and, in southern France, Côtes du Ventoux.

Grenache is also found in most of Provence's table wine. In Roussillon it is, perhaps surprisingly, an ingredient of the *Vins Doux Naturels* such as Banyuls and Rivesaltes; Rasteau in the Côtes du Rhône is another such example.

NEW WORLD Although Grenache is widely grown in Australia, its popularity there is on the wane, except arguably in the Barossa Valley. Nowadays, much Australian Grenache goes into jug wines.

Until the early 1990s, Grenache was the third most planted red grape in California (after Cabernet Sauvignon and Zinfandel), and it is still popular there. It was mainly used to make port-style wines, but has recently been transformed into southern Rhône-style reds by producers such as Joseph Phelps, Preston Vineyards, Quivira, McDowell Valley Vineyards and Bonny Doon.

SPAIN As Spain's most widespread red grape, Garnacha (as Grenache is known there) is grown mainly in Rioja, Navarra, Cariñena, La Mancha, Penedès, Priorato, Tarragona, Terra Alta and Utiel-Requena. It is used on its own, as in Navarra for example, or in blends, as in Rioja, where it provides the body and finesse needed to temper the more austere Tempranillo. Unblended Garnacha has low tannin, high alcohol and an underlying sweetness.

MERLOT

(Synonym: Merlot Noir)

MAINLY GROWN IN Bordeaux, California, Chile, and central and northeast Italy.

ALSO GROWN IN Argentina, Australia, Bulgaria, Hungary, New Zealand, Romania, South Africa, Switzerland and Washington State.

STYLE Early yielding and early ripening, Merlot produces wines that are plump, luscious and full-flavoured, noted for their aromas of black cherries, blackcurrants, plums, vanilla, pepper, toffee and mint.

WINES Any country that grows Cabernet Sauvignon is likely to grow Merlot too. The grape ripens earlier than Cabernet Sauvignon, producing lower levels of tannin but higher levels of sugar, a combination that results in softer wines with slightly higher degrees of alcohol.

As a consequence, Merlots tend to be more supple and rounded than Cabernet Sauvignons, but less complex and profound – meaning that they can be drunk when they're younger but they won't last for quite as long. Cabernet Sauvignon and Cabernet Franc are often blended with Merlot to give it more structure.

BORDEAUX Merlot is a vital component in the blends that make claret. In the Médoc, it plays second fiddle to the dominant Cabernet Sauvignon, but it is still important as it softens the latter's harder edges. In St-Emilion, Pomerol and Fronsac, however,

Merlot plays by far the greater role, as evidenced by Pomerol's illustrious Château Pétrus, which is made almost entirely from Merlot.

CALIFORNIA In the New World, Merlot is sometimes used on its own to make wines of great style. As a rule, California Merlots are more dense than those of Bordeaux. When not made into single varietals, the grape is often used in the highest-quality blends, such as Mondavi-Rothschild's Opus One and Joseph Phelps's Insignia. While some argue that America's best Merlots come from Washington State (Chateau Ste-Michelle is especially sought after), the grape is increasingly popular in California, with Duckhorn Vineyards, Firestone, Beringer, Ferrari-Carano, Matanzas Creek and Arrowood all making fine single varietals.

CHILE Chilean Merlots have come on in leaps and bounds in recent years. They tend to taste full and fresh, with good black-fruit flavour, and are considered some to be superior to the country's Cabernet Sauvignon.

ITALY Merlot is especially popular in Friuli-Venezia Giulia, Emilia-Romagna, Trentino-Alto Adige and the Veneto. Together with Sangiovese and Cabernet Sauvignon, it is often a component of the rich and concentrated "Super Tuscan" wines. At its lowest level, however, Italian Merlot can be frustratingly thin, light and often bitter.

PINOT NOIR

(Synonyms: Blauburgunder, Blauer Spätburgunder, Pineau, Pinot Nero, Spätburgunder)

MAINLY GROWN IN Burgundy, California, Champagne, Eastern Europe, New Zealand, Oregon, Victoria and Western Australia.

ALSO GROWN IN Alsace, Germany, Jura and the Loire.

STYLE Pinot Noir is something of a chameleon when it comes to flavour. When young, its wines smell of cherries, plums, raspberries and strawberries; when mature, they take on complex aromas of chocolate, game, rotting vegetables, prunes, truffles and violets. Old Pinot from Burgundy is often characterised by a "farmyard" smell – rather more appealing than it sounds.

WINES Pinot Noir is a so-and-so of a grape to grow because it ripens early and is susceptible to frost damage. Nevertheless, it does beautifully in France, especially in Burgundy. The grape has been less successful outside France than other classic grape varieties, although some exciting wines are now being made from it in other parts of the world. Unlike Cabernet Sauvignon, which retains its characteristics wherever it is grown, Pinot Noir can taste very different from one environment to the next.

BURGUNDY Pinot Noir flourishes nowhere as well as it does in Burgundy, where (unblended) it makes the region's finest red wines, such as Clos de Vougeot, Corton, Beaune, Gevrey-Chambertin, Nuits-St-Georges, Pommard and Romanée-Conti.

Burgundy's red wines, with the exception of Beaujolais, rare red Mâcon and Passetoutgrains, are all made from Pinot Noir, and the quality can vary dramatically.

CHAMPAGNE Pinot Noir plays an important role in Champagne, where it is blended with Chardonnay and Pinot Meunier to make the world's most celebrated sparkling wine. Infrequently, certain producers make (white) champagne, known as *blanc de noirs,* solely from Pinot Noir.

OTHER FRENCH REGIONS Pinot Noir is also grown with some success in the Loire, where it is responsible for the delightful, light and charming red and rosé Sancerres, and in Alsace, where its wine is highly regarded locally, although rarely seen abroad.

OTHER EUROPE In Germany, Pinot Noir produces a light, almost rosé, style of wine that is difficult for outsiders to appreciate, while in Hungary the same grape is used to make wines of surprising (some would say overwhelming) sweetness.

NEW WORLD The cool climates of regions such as Oregon, Victoria and Western Australia are ideal for producing vibrant wines with plenty of raspberry-like fruit, while New Zealand's Pinot Noirs tend to show jammy, cherry flavours with a back note of subtle oak – watch out especially for wines made in Martinborough and Central Otago.

SANGIOVESE

(Synonyms: Brunello, Calabrese, Prugnolo)

MAINLY GROWN IN Italy.

ALSO GROWN IN Argentina and California.

STYLE A slow and late ripener, Sangiovese can make deliciously fruity wines which are rich and alcoholic in good years, and which can have upfront tannin and acidity when young. The grape's flavour varies wildly from wine to wine, but usually boasts an earthy tone. Unfortunately, Sangiovese is prone to oxidisation.

WINES Sangiovese-based wines are not deeply coloured and can often be recognised in the glass by a tell-tale orange tinge at the rim. Despite the grape's proliferation in Italy, the quality of its wines can vary from sublime to sludge, mainly because there are so many different varietal clones.

There are two major subvarieties: Sangiovese Grosso and Sangiovese Piccolo. The former is grown mainly in Tuscany to great acclaim, while the latter is grown mainly in Emilia-Romagna to deafening silence.

ITALY The main grape of Chianti, Brunello di Montalcino and Vino Nobile di Montepulciano, Sangiovese is the most widely planted red grape in Italy and is concentrated in the central and southern regions. It may well be cock-of-the-walk in Chianti, but it is also responsible for some very ordinary wines in the Marches, Umbria and Latium.

Sangiovese undoubtedly makes the best red wines of Tuscany: traditional ones as well as the so-called "Super Tuscans". It provides up to 90 per cent of the Chianti blend (the remainder being made up of Canaiolo, Colorino, Mammolo and the white grapes Trebbiano or Malvasia), and up to 80 per cent of the Vino Nobile di Montepulciano blend (the wine is named after the town of Montepulciano, by the way, not after the grape of the same name). Brunello di Montalcino, on the other hand, is unblended Sangiovese: a deep, rich and full-flavoured wine which, unlike most examples of the variety, ages well; the most famous and long-lived example is made by Biondi-Santi. Sangiovese goes remarkably well with Cabernet Sauvignon and Merlot, and such blends form the basis of many "Super Tuscans". Antinori's famous Tignanello, for example, is a Sangiovese-Cabernet Sauvignon blend.

NEW WORLD Although Sangiovese is rarely seen outside Italy, there are plantings in the Mendoza province of Argentina. Following the success of the "Super Tuscans", producers in California began to investigate Sangiovese's potential, planting it in the Napa Valley (where Atlas Peak Vineyards makes a fine single varietal), Sonoma County, San Luis Obispo County and the Sierra Foothills.

SYRAH

(Synonyms: Marsanne Noir, Shiraz, Sirac)

MAINLY GROWN IN Australia and the Rhône.

ALSO GROWN IN Argentina, California, the Midi, Morocco and South Africa.

STYLE When young, Syrah gives off aromas of pepper, spice and even tar, to which are added blackberries, blackcurrants, plums and leather as it ages. In colour, it is invariably a deep, almost opaque, red, while on the palate it is big, full, rich, jammy and spicy.

WINES Syrah is responsible for some of the world's great wines, most notably Côte-Rôtie and Hermitage in the northern Rhône and Penfolds Grange in Australia. Syrah is easy to grow, produces a reliable crop and is resistant to most pests and diseases, thriving especially well in poor soils and warm climates. Owing to Syrah's high tannin levels, wines made from the grape age remarkably well, the top ones taking many years to mature.

AUSTRALIA Syrah, known in Australia as Shiraz, arrived in the country in the 1830s and is now the most planted variety there, achieving its greatest successes in the Hunter and Barossa Valleys and in Coonawarra. It is frequently blended with Cabernet Sauvignon, giving the latter variety body and backbone and resulting in wines of lip-smacking juiciness, with a hint of chocolate and minerals, and a tang of "sweaty saddles".

Although widely used to produce everyday jug wines, Shiraz is also used to make sparkling and fortified wines – try Seppelts Show Sparkling Shiraz, for example.

FRANCE In the northern Rhône, where Syrah is the dominant grape variety, it is cultivated on precipitous granite slopes and yields dense, dark, full-bodied, concentrated wines of massive smoky, tarry flavour, such as Cornas, Côte-Rôtie, Hermitage and the lighter Crozes-Hermitage and St-Joseph. Owing to the grape's intensity, a dash of the white Viognier grape is often added to Côte-Rôtie to give it an element of softness and a distinctive perfume. Hermitage and Côte-Rôtie are extremely long-lived; Cornas, too, needs time to reach its best. Crozes-Hermitage and St-Joseph can be enjoyed earlier – usually within five years. In the southern Rhône, where Grenache rules the roost, Syrah adds structure, flavour and zip to Châteauneuf-du-Pape as one of the wine's 13 permitted grape varieties. The Midi has jumped on the Syrah bandwagon with as much keenness as it has for the other major varietals, making good-value, soft, gluggable wines.

NEW WORLD Syrah is now being planted with increasing frequency in California, either for use in Rhône-style blends or as single varietals, most successfully by Joseph Phelps (who has cultivated it since 1974). South America and South Africa are also starting to show their potential for making juicy, spicy styles of Syrah.

BARBERA

(No synonyms)

MAINLY GROWN IN Northwest Italy.

ALSO GROWN IN Argentina, Australia, Brazil, California and Uruguay.

STYLE High in rich forest fruit and acidity, low in tannin.

WINES Barbera makes sound purple-coloured wines with fresh acidity, bags of raisiny fruit and a dry finish. They need little ageing and are a pleasure. Barbera makes northwest Italy's everyday wines – a more quaffable proposition than Nebbiolo – as well as rosés and sparkling wines which can be sweet or dry.

ITALY A relatively late-ripening grape, Barbera is one of the most prolific grape varieties in Italy, with only Nebbiolo and Sangiovese as its rivals. It is grown chiefly in Piemonte, Lombardy and Emilia-Romagna. The best-known wines are Piemonte's Barbera d'Alba, Barbera d'Asti and Barbera del Monferrato (the latter often including other varieties).

NEW WORLD In hotter regions, Barbera's high alcohol and good acidity levels make it suitable for blending, which is why it appears in Argentina, California and Australia, giving cheaper blends a firmer dimension.

CABERNET FRANC

(Synonyms: Bordo, Bouchet, Breton, Cabernet Frank, Carmenet, Trouchet Noir)

MAINLY GROWN IN Bordeaux, the Loire and northeast Italy.

ALSO GROWN IN Argentina, California, New York, New Zealand and Washington State.

STYLE Cabernet Franc is a less tannic, less full-bodied, but more aromatic version of Cabernet Sauvignon.

WINES Usually a junior partner in claret blends, it also makes fine Loire reds.

BORDEAUX Its starring role is in St-Emilion, where it makes lush blends. It is often used

to boost the flavour of Cabernet Sauvignon, and is favoured for its early ripening. The wines are herbaceous in style.

LOIRE Cool conditions promote vibrant red wines such as Bourgueil and Chinon, and the charming rosé, Cabernet d'Anjou.

ITALY Much of what passes for Cabernet Sauvignon in Italy is in fact Cabernet Franc, making light, soft, early-drinking wines.

NEW WORLD Generally it is only grown in small amounts, usually for "Meritage" blends. Australia produces a few single varietals.

CARIGNAN

(Synonyms: Carignane, Carignan Noir, Cariñena, Mazuelo, Monestel)

MAINLY GROWN IN Languedoc-Roussillon and Spain.

ALSO GROWN IN Argentina, California, Chile, Italy, Israel, Mexico and Uruguay.

STYLE This thick-skinned grape produces deep-coloured wines that are high in tannin and alcohol and are ideal for blending.

WINES A late-ripener, Carignan does well in hot climates. It is widely planted.

LANGUEDOC-ROUSSILLON Carignan has long dominated this area, especially in the Aude,

Hérault, Gard and Pyrénées-Orientales regions. Less in favour nowadays, many of its vines are being uprooted. At its best it is fruity and spicy; at its worst, inoffensive and dull. Carignan is a component of Minervois, Corbières, Fitou and Provençal rosés, and blends with Cinsault in the western Midi and Grenache in the eastern Midi.

SPAIN Carignan is thought to have originated in the Cariñena area of northern Spain, where it makes deep-coloured, full-bodied and robust table wines that are strong in alcohol and tannin. It also adds colour and body to Rioja.

GAMAY

(Synonyms: Gamay Noir à Jus Blanc, Petit Gamai)

MAINLY GROWN IN Beaujolais and the Loire.

ALSO GROWN IN California and Switzerland.

STYLE Pale red in colour, high in acidity, low in tannin, light, fresh and fruity.

WINES Gamay is used to make Beaujolais. Other than scatterings in Switzerland (where it is usually blended with Pinot Noir), it is largely disregarded by the rest of Europe.

FRANCE All Beaujolais is made from Gamay, and it is in this region that the grape is at its best. It should be undemanding to drink,

with no disconcerting complexities: just fresh, juicy fruit flavours and seductive aromas of cherries and berries. Most Beaujolais is best drunk young, although the top *crus* do have some capacity to age. Gamay is also grown in Burgundy's Mâconnais and Côte Chalonnaise, and combines with Pinot Noir to make Bourgogne Passe-Tout-Grains. In the Loire it can be used to make Anjou Rosé, Anjou Gamay and Gamay de Touraine.

CALIFORNIA Chiefly Beaujolais Nouveau-style wines, but some are full-bodied and oak-aged. The grapes known as Napa Gamay and Gamay Beaujolais are different varieties.

MALBEC

(Synonyms: Auxerrois, Cot, Malbeck, Pressac)

MAINLY GROWN IN Argentina, Chile and France (Bordeaux, Cahors and the Loire).

ALSO GROWN IN California, northeast Italy.

STYLE Malbec is a black-skinned, spicy, juicy, early-ripening grape which produces soft, blackberryish, quick-maturing wines that are low in acidity.

WINES Once an essential ingredient in claret blends, it has recently fallen out of fashion.

FRANCE Malbec's low acidity and softness make it ideal for combining with Cabernet Sauvignon, but the only areas of Bordeaux that continue to hold it in esteem are Bourg and Blaye. It is still well thought of in Cahors (southwest France), where it is blended with Merlot and Tannat to make the region's fabled fiery "black wine". It is also grown in the Loire for blending with Gamay and Cabernet Franc.

SOUTH AMERICA Malbec is the second most planted grape variety in Argentina, where it is used to make the country's top red wines. It is also widely grown in Chile, where it is used for blending with Merlot and Petit Verdot.

MOURVEDRE

(Synonyms: Balzac, Mataro, Monastrell)

MAINLY GROWN IN Southern France, Spain.

ALSO GROWN IN Australia and California.

STYLE Heady, garnet-coloured wines with spicy, peppery characteristics and aromas of blackberries. Best when blended.

WINES Thought to have originated in Spain, (where it is known as Monastrell). Mourvèdre is an essential ingredient in the southern Rhône's Châteauneuf-du-Pape.

SOUTHERN FRANCE Not as widely planted as Syrah, Grenache or Cinsault (with which it is usually blended), it is an essential ingredient in many wines – Bandol (the rosé, too), Cassis and Palette; it also boosts the flavour and improves the colour of Corbières, Côtes du Roussillon, Côtes du Rhône-Villages and Côtes de Provence.

SPAIN An important variety, prevalent in Valencia and Alicante, where it is made into dark, mostly dry, alcoholic reds and rosés.

NEW WORLD California grows a little, and Australia (where it is known as Mataro) blends it with Shiraz to make port styles.

NEBBIOLO

(Synonyms: Spanna, Picotener, Pugnet)

MAINLY GROWN IN Northwest Italy.

ALSO GROWN IN Argentina, California, Mexico and Switzerland.

STYLE Nebbiolo makes dark, chewy, tannic wines, which are high in alcohol and fierce when young. With age it mellows into flavours and aromas of liquorice, prunes and chocolate.

WINES Nebbiolo makes the big, tannic wines of Piemonte.

ITALY Although capable of producing complex and intense wines, Nebbiolo is only grown in quantity in northwest Italy. Barolo and Barbaresco are made solely from Nebbiolo, while Gattinara, Ghemme and Spanna are all based on the grape. Nebbiolo wines usually need plenty of ageing, although modern winemaking techniques have resulted in slightly softer wines full of rich, velvety fruit.

REST OF WORLD While some plantings do exist in Argentina, California and Switzerland, they do not produce wines with anything like the quality of those from Piemonte.

PETIT VERDOT

(Synonyms: Carmelin, Petit Verdau, Verdot, Verdot Rouge)

MAINLY GROWN IN Bordeaux.

ALSO GROWN IN California and Chile.

STYLE Petit Verdot makes full-bodied, deep-coloured wines that are high in tannin and alcohol and have peppery, spicy flavours.

WINES Traditionally used in tiny amounts to add colour, tannin and flavour to claret.

BORDEAUX Petit Verdot is a high-quality, thick-skinned grape not dissimilar to Syrah. It is little seen outside Bordeaux, and even there its main role is that of a flavour enhancer to the Bordeaux blends. It imparts a delightful spicy herbiness to these wines, but never comprises more than 10 per cent. Petit Verdot is used chiefly in the southern Médoc, where the soil produces light wines that tend to be in need of a flavour boost. However, it ripens late (in inferior vintages it never ripens at all) and is a poor cropper, making it hard to rely on and therefore a luxury that few growers can afford.

REST OF WORLD Small amounts of Petit Verdot are grown in California and Chile, where it is also used to add spice and seasoning to blended wines.

PINOTAGE

(No synonyms)

MAINLY GROWN IN South Africa.

ALSO GROWN IN California and New Zealand.

STYLE Pinotage produces fruity, medium-bodied wines which are usually dark purple in colour and high in tannin and acid.

WINES Pinotage is a cross between Pinot Noir and Cinsaut. It can make fresh, fruity wines and wines for ageing, but it rarely makes wines that are as good as those made by either of its parents.

SOUTH AFRICA A dramatic increase in plantings has occured here, due to South Africa's pride in its "own" grape variety. Many producers believe that it should be drunk young, while fresh and Beaujolais-like, but others make deep, brooding styles with firm tannins and acidity for mellowing with age.

REST OF WORLD California and New Zealand are both starting to dabble with this grape variety, with varied results. As in South Africa, badly made Pinotage appears flabby and dull and smells of burnt rubber and drains.

PINOT MEUNIER

(Synonyms: Meunier, Miller's Burgundy, Müllerrebe, Plant Meunier, Schwarzriesling)

MAINLY GROWN IN Champagne.

ALSO GROWN IN Australia, California, Germany and Switzerland.

STYLE A reliably productive variety, producing wines full of fruitiness and high acidity.

WINES Its main role is to partner Pinot Noir and Chardonnay in the champagne blends. It withstands spring frosts, which makes it particularly well suited to cool regions.

CHAMPAGNE Pinot Meunier is, surprisingly, the most widely planted grape variety in

Champagne. Its job here is to add fresh fruitiness and crisp acidity to champagne blends – complementing the weight of Pinot Noir (to which it is distantly related) and the refinement of Chardonnay. Pinot Meunier is far less glamorous than these two grapes, and so much less fuss is made of it, despite the fact that it is used more widely.

REST OF WORLD Pinot Meunier is scarcely seen outside Champagne, although it is grown in Germany, Switzerland, California, and Australia (probably the only country to use it to make single-varietal wines).

TEMPRANILLO

(Synonyms: Aragonez, Cencibel, Tinta del Pais, Tinto Fino, Tinta Roriz, Ull de Llebre)

MAINLY GROWN IN Spain.

ALSO GROWN IN Argentina, France and Portugal.

STYLE Good colour, fine ageing potential and firm acidity. Herbal, spicy, sour cherry and summer fruit with hints of tobacco.

WINES Tempranillo makes a range of wines, from light to robust, and is best known for providing backbone to the wines of Rioja.

SPAIN Tempranillo is made into single varietals or blended, as in Rioja, with Garnacha, Mazuelo, Viura and Graciano. In Ribera del Duero it helps to make Spain's finest wine: Vega Sicilia. It is the dominant red variety in Valdepeñas and La Mancha and is grown in Costers del Segre, Utiel-Requena, Somontano, Penedès, Toro, Navarra and Catalonia.

REST OF WORLD Tempranillo is grown in the Midi in France, and in Portugal where, known as Tinta Roriz, it is an ingredient in port. It is also successful in the Mendoza region of Argentina and may well be California's Valdepeñas grape variety, used in the production of jug wine.

ZINFANDEL

(Synonyms: possibly Primitivo, Primativo – Italy)

MAINLY GROWN IN California.

ALSO GROWN IN Australia, Italy, South Africa and South America.

STYLE Makes red, white or rosé wines; lightish, full or fortified; bone-dry or bubblegum sweet; still or sparkling. Flavours include berry fruits, plums and spice.

WINES Top wines are full-bodied and masculine.

CALIFORNIA Zinfandel produces robust, spicy reds whose uncomplicated fruitiness can make them easy to drink. But their firm structure also gives them the potential to age and trends are seeing a rise in alcohol levels, with some being too high for export laws. Most successful commercially, however, are the blush-wines, the so-called "white Zinfandels", which are great summertime gluggers for lovers of candyfloss. Zinfandel is also used in blended port styles.

ITALY Known as Primitivo, in the south it is made into interesting sweet or dry styles.

AUSTRALIA A few producers, in particular Cape Mentelle and Nepenthe, make sturdy, long-lived stunners.

white grapes

CHARDONNAY

(Synonyms: Beaunois, Chardennet, Chardenai, Gamay Blanc, Pinot Chardonnay)

MAINLY GROWN IN Australia, Bulgaria, Burgundy, California, Central Europe, Chablis, Champagne, Chile, Italy, New Zealand and South Africa.

ALSO GROWN IN Canada, New York, Oregon, Spain and just about everywhere that grapes are grown.

STYLE Typical flavours associated with Chardonnay include butter, cream, nuts, apple, lemon, melon and pineapple. When oaked, Chardonnay takes on a deeper colour and fuller, softer, vanilla and coconut flavours. Pure Chardonnay wines tend to have good acidity levels and high alcohol potential and, to top it off, Chardonnay ages well. Its flavours change dramatically from region to region, and even from district to district within the same region.

WINES Chardonnay is the dominant element in Champagne, and the only grape of the great white wines of Burgundy, such as Corton-Charlemagne, Meursault, Montrachet and Pouilly-Fuissé. It makes top-quality, single varietal wines and blends in the New World as well as regular quaffing wine. It is difficult to make a bad wine from Chardonnay, whether on its own or blended with other grape varieties, whose qualities it has the uncanny ability to enhance.

AMERICA Chardonnay is virtually synonymous with white wine here, being regarded almost as a generic name. It is especially beloved in California, where it makes wines of great style, power and complexity – unfortunately, sometimes with prices to match – with hints of vanilla and almonds.

AUSTRALIA Although producers have triumphantly pioneered Chardonnay/Semillon blends, their greatest successes remain the massive, tropical fruit-flavoured single varietals. These wines are widely admired, although some wine-lovers consider them over-dependent on oak.

BURGUNDY All but the humblest white burgundies are made entirely from Chardonnay, and Chablis is only ever made from Chardonnay. Throughout Burgundy the grape produces buttery wines, but in Chablis it is more steely, in Meursault more pineappley and in Mâcon more flinty.

CHAMPAGNE Most is a blend of Chardonnay and the red grapes Pinot Noir and Pinot Meunier; the proportion of the blend differs from producer to producer. A few champagnes, labelled *blanc de blancs*, are made solely from Chardonnay.

CHENIN BLANC

(Synonyms: Pineau d'Anjou, Pineau de la Loire, Steen)

MAINLY GROWN IN: California, the Loire, New Zealand and South Africa.

ALSO GROWN IN Argentina, Australia, Brazil, Chile and Mexico.

STYLE It yields wines of high acidity with the ability to age for many years. At its most basic level, Chenin Blanc is light, dry and fresh, with restrained aromas of citrus fruit, apple and melon. At its most opulent, it has aromas of damp straw and rich honey.

WINES Chenin Blanc is one of the world's most versatile grape varieties, capable of producing light, dry, everyday drinking wine; sparkling wine; fine, long-lived sweet wines; and even – notably in South Africa – fortified wines and spirits. Its real home is in the Loire, where it gets the most respect, while in the New World it is often used simply for blending into commercial wines.

CALIFORNIA This state plants more Chenin Blanc than France. The variety is grown mainly in the hot Central Valley and is used to make a base wine for commercial blends. Given the American palate's preference for Chardonnay and Sauvignon, even the best Chenin rarely gets a look in, although some producers, such as Chappellet Vineyards, make a single varietal Chenin Blanc.

LOIRE Chenin Blanc shows just how adaptable it can be in the Loire, where it flies solo in the best wines, but often rubs shoulders with Chardonnay or Sauvignon Blanc in blends. Its high acidity makes it ideal for producing sparkling wines such as sparkling Saumur. Chenin Blanc also makes dry to medium-dry Anjou Blanc and Savennières (the finest, most elegant example), while in Touraine it produces dry, medium, sweet or sparkling Vouvray. It is also used to make wines of intense, honeyed sweetness such as Côteaux du Layon. In poor summers, Chenin Blanc's high acidity can work against it, resulting in wines that are too sharp and green to be enjoyable. The most celebrated Chenin Blancs in the Loire are the sweet late-picked styles, which are already high in natural sugar due to time spent ripening in the sun; this sweetness is further increased in some areas by the presence of botrytis.

AUSTRALIA AND NEW ZEALAND Chenin Blanc is popular in the Poverty Bay and Hawke's Bay areas and makes fine sweet wines. In both New Zealand and Australia, Chenin Blanc is aged regularly in new oak barrels, a rare occurrence in the Loire.

SOUTH AFRICA A country which grows three times as much Chenin Blanc (or Steen, as it's known here) as France. It uses the variety chiefly for making light, spritzy, off-dry wines that are refreshing and high in acidity but with little character. However, this is beginning to change as producers get to grips with international markets.

RIESLING

(Synonyms: Johannisberger, Johannisberg Riesling, Rhine Riesling, Weisser Riesling)

MAINLY GROWN IN Alsace, Australia and Germany.

ALSO GROWN IN Argentina, Austria, California, Canada, Chile, Italy, New Zealand, New York, Ontario, Oregon, South Africa and Washington State.

STYLE Pale in colour, Riesling (pronounced Reezling, not Ryzling) is recognisable by its striking aroma of honey, apples, citrus fruit, apricots, pineapples, peaches and, above all, petrol – and fully leaded petrol at that. It plays to its strengths, uniting crisp acidity and high sugar levels to make fascinating wines capable of lasting for decades.

WINES Ignore Welschriesling, Cape Riesling, Emerald Riesling, Gray Riesling and Paarl Riesling – they are all different grape varieties. Riesling is the real McCoy, Germany's finest and Chardonnay's only rival as the world's greatest white grape, winning on versatility if not popularity. It can make anything from bone-dry wines to intensely sweet ones – either late-picked or affected by botrytis.

ALSACE Riesling plays a vital role here, where it is regarded as top dog by the producers (if not always by the consumers). Here it results in weightier, drier and more alcoholic wines than its Germanic counterparts.

AUSTRALIA The biggest grower of Riesling (where it is known as Rhine Riesling) in the New World. The grape is mainly in the Barossa, Eden and Clare valleys, where the wines are usually higher in body and alcohol than most European Rieslings.

AUSTRIA Produces dry, concentrated wines.

CALIFORNIA Most of the state is too warm to produce dry Riesling, so delicious late-harvest wines of intense sweetness are made instead, notably in Monterey, Santa Barbara and Mendocino.

GERMANY Riesling is *the* grape of Germany, and its prime site is the northern Mosel-Saar-Ruwer region; many top estates here grow practically nothing else. The other great areas include the Rheingau, Pfalz and Württemberg. German Rieslings tend to be low in alcohol, ranging in style and quality from dryish to tooth-shakingly sweet. They can be delightfully refreshing, especially in the garden on a summer evening.

ITALY Riesling is particularly successful in the Friuli-Venezia Giulia and Trentino-Alto Adige regions, and in the latter it makes particularly delicate and aromatic wines.

NEW ZEALAND Look out for attractive crisp, elegant styles from Marlborough.

WASHINGTON STATE AND ONTARIO Cool conditions produce wines of great delicacy, including the superb Canadian speciality Icewine, made from frozen grapes.

SAUVIGNON BLANC

(Synonyms: Blanc Fumé, Fumé Blanc, Sauvignon Jaune)

MAINLY GROWN IN Bordeaux, California, Loire and New Zealand.

ALSO GROWN IN Australia, Eastern Europe, Italy, South Africa, South America and Spain.

STYLE Sauvignon Blanc is easily identifiable on the nose by its aromas of gooseberry, blackcurrant leaf, nettles, cut grass and cat's pee (honestly). It can make light, dry, zesty, refreshing wines for early drinking and full-bodied dry or sweet wines for ageing.

WINES Unblended, Sauvignon Blanc is responsible for such famous wines as Sancerre and Pouilly-Fumé from the Loire. Combined with Sémillon, it makes the great dry wines of Pessac-Léognan and the celebrated dessert wines of Sauternes and Barsac.

BORDEAUX Producers frequently blend Sauvignon Blanc with Sémillon, the latter variety smoothing out Sauvignon's sharper edges and helping the wine to age well. Many of these blended wines spend time in oak, too, where they take on additional depth of flavour. The grapes produce the easy-drinking, dry white wines of Entre-Deux-Mers as well as the top-quality dry wines of Pessac-Léognan. Sauvignon Blanc also plays a small but important part in the dessert wines of Monbazillac, Loupiac, Sauternes and Barsac, where it is added, often with a dash of Muscadelle, to the Sémillon-dominated blends.

CALIFORNIA It was Robert Mondavi who pioneered the production of Sauvignon Blanc in California, succeeding not only in making delicious wine but also in selling it to initially sceptical consumers. His decision to market his wines under the name "Fumé Blanc" rather than "Sauvignon Blanc" struck a chord with Americans, who found the name more user-friendly and easier to pronounce. The result is that Sauvignon Blanc is nearly as popular a variety in California as Chardonnay. As in Bordeaux, California producers often use oak to add richness to their wines.

LOIRE Sauvignon Blanc is often called Blanc Fumé in the Loire. Producers don't believe in blending it with other varieties; instead, they use it to make single varietal wines that are fermented and aged in stainless-steel vats to retain their crisp and clean primary fruit characteristics. While Sancerre and Pouilly-Fumé are the most sought-after Sauvignons of the region, Quincy, Reuilly, Menetou-Salon and even the basic Sauvignon de Touraine are also fine examples.

NEW ZEALAND Sauvignon Blancs, especially from Marlborough, took the world by storm modelling themselves on the best Sancerres and Pouilly-Fumés of the Loire, eschewing wood in favour of the purity gained by vinification and ageing in steel. They are now considered to be among the finest Sauvignon Blancs in the world.

SEMILLON

(Synonyms: Chevrier, Hunter River Riesling, Sémillon Blanc)

MAINLY GROWN IN America, Australia and Bordeaux.

ALSO GROWN IN Argentina, Chile, eastern Europe, New Zealand and South Africa.

STYLE Sémillon produces big, waxy, lemony, flavour-packed wines that age particularly well, especially in oak. They tend to be dark yellow in colour, low in acidity, rich and full-bodied. Notable aromas include pears, honey, apples and nuts.

Sémillon has a tendency to be a touch one-dimensional when unblended, but when combined with Sauvignon Blanc it can make some of the finest white wines in the world. Sauvignon brings high alcohol and acidity to the marriage, while Sémillon offers soft flavours and richness to combat its partner's inclination to grassiness. It could be argued that, when brought together, these two grapes make better wines than either does on its own.

WINES Sémillon is best known for producing powerful single varietals in Australia's Hunter Valley and, blended with Sauvignon Blanc, for producing the intensely sweet wines of Sauternes and Barsac.

AMERICA The best Sémillons in America hail from the Pacific Northwest (Washington's Hogue Cellars, for example). The grape is also widely grown in California, notably in Livermore Valley, Napa Valley, Sonoma County and Santa Ynez Valley, and is used largely for combining with Sauvignon Blanc in the so-called "Meritage" blends.

AUSTRALIA (Where Semillon loses the acute on its "e".) The grape is widely grown, especially in New South Wales. Although its traditional blending partner in France is Sauvignon Blanc, the Australians have had great success in matching Semillon with Chardonnay, particularly in the Barossa and Hunter Valleys, where for a long time the grape was known as Hunter Riesling. It is also in Australia that Semillon is at its best as a single varietal, contradicting those (so the producers would argue) who believe that unblended Semillon cannot make great wine.

BORDEAUX Sémillon is the most widely planted white grape variety by far, and is used to make anything from basic white Bordeaux (either unblended or with Sauvignon Blanc, Ugni Blanc or Colombard) to the top-quality dry white wines of Pessac-Léognan in conjunction with Sauvignon Blanc. However, its greatest success in the region lies in Sauternes and Barsac, where its lusciousness and susceptibility to botrytis make it ideal for creating the finest dessert wines. It is usually blended with up to 20 per cent Sauvignon Blanc, and perhaps a small amount of Muscadelle, to produce sweet wines of intense, honeyed complexity and richness, that age beautifully.

ALIGOTE

(Synonyms: Blanc de Troyes, Chaudenet Gras, Plant Gris)

MAINLY GROWN IN Burgundy.

ALSO GROWN IN Bulgaria, California, Chile, Romania and Russia.

STYLE Fresh, acidic white wines, often with pleasant hints of lemon and lime, which are best drunk young.

WINES Great as the base for Kir, a traditional drink using *crème de cassis*. Despite the fact that Aligoté has been grown in Burgundy for centuries, it has long been regarded as "the poor man's Chardonnay", lacking the latter's depth of flavour and ageing potential.

BURGUNDY Bourgogne Aligoté de Bouzeron, is an unexciting example of the grape at its limited best. Although Aligoté is making way for new plantings of Chardonnay throughout much of Burgundy, Bourgogne Aligoté continues to provide much of the everyday drinking wine in this region.

REST OF WORLD Aligoté retains its popularity in Eastern Europe. It remains Russia's second most-planted grape variety, where it is one of the constituents of its sparkling wine. Apart from small amounts grown in California and Chile, it is little seen in the New World.

GEWURZTRAMINER

(Synonyms: Klevner, Traminer, Gris Rouge)

MAINLY GROWN IN Alsace.

ALSO GROWN IN Australia, Austria, British Columbia, California, Chile, Germany, Italy, New Zealand, Oregon, Washington State.

STYLE The most gloriously flamboyant of all grapes, with a pungent aroma – often likened to lychees, grapefruit, rose petals and spice – which leaps out and zaps you on the hooter.

WINES An unforgettable flavour. The word Gewürz means "spice" in German, but the variety is thought to have originated in Italy's Alto Adige. It likes cool climates best.

ALSACE Most at home here (where it loses its umlaut), the grape makes not only remarkably perfumed dry wines but also stunningly intense and sweet *vendanges tardives* and *sélections des grains nobles*.

NEW WORLD In Australia it is grown with great success by Delatite, in Central Victoria. It is also grown in the cooler areas of California, where it makes scented and soft wines. But, of all New World countries, the grape is at its happiest in New Zealand – most notably in Gisborne, where Matawhero makes some of the country's finest examples.

MULLER-THURGAU

(Synonyms: Riesling-Silvaner, Rivaner)

MAINLY GROWN IN Germany, New Zealand.

ALSO GROWN IN Austria, England, Hungary, northeast Italy, Slovenia and Switzerland.

STYLE Light and fruity to bland and tasteless.

WINES A Riesling/Silvaner hybrid cross.

GERMANY Liebfraumilch is Müller-Thurgau's most famous incarnation – heaven help it.

NEW ZEALAND Makes impressive varietals.

OTHER OLD WORLD Clean wines from Austria and Italy's Trentino-Alto Adige. It is England's most widely planted variety.

MARSANNE

(Synonyms: Ermitage Blanc, Grosse Roussette, Hermitage Blanc)

MAINLY GROWN IN Rhône.

ALSO GROWN IN Algeria, Australia, California, southern France and Switzerland.

STYLE Deep-coloured wines which are high in alcohol and have distinctive, heady orchard fruit, nuts, spice and almonds.

WINES Both fruity, perfumed early drinking wines and oaky, long-ageing styles.

RHÔNE Various dry styles, north and south.

REST OF WORLD Known as Ermitage Blanc in Switzerland. It makes some impressive, top-quality styles in Australia and California.

MUSCAT

(Synonyms: Frontignac, Moscato, Moscatel, Muscadel, Muscatel, Muskateller, Muskuti, Tamyanka)

MAINLY GROWN IN Australia, France, Greece, Italy, Portugal and Spain.

ALSO GROWN IN North America and in small quantities in many wine regions of the world.

STYLE The only wines that taste of grapes. Makes mainly sweet but some dry wines.

WINES The oldest grape variety known.

FRANCE Muscat de Beaumes-de-Venise and sparklers in the Rhône, dry styles in the south.

OTHER Asti in Italy; Samos in Greece; dry in Alsace and Austria; sweet Moscatel wines in Spain and Portugal. Sweet in Australia and US.

PINOT BLANC

(Synonyms: Pinot Bianco, Weisser Burgunder, Weissburgunder)

MAINLY GROWN IN Alsace, Austria, Germany and Italy.

ALSO GROWN IN Burgundy, California, Chile, Luxembourg, Uruguay and Eastern Europe.

STYLE Fresh, yeasty, appley aroma, with high acidity and crispness – ideal for making refreshing still and sparkling wines.

WINES Best known in Alsace.

ALSACE Made as a single varietal, producers such as Hugel, Cave Vinicole de Turckheim and Kreydenweiss transform it into very drinkable wine.

OTHER OLD WORLD Burgundy grows a little to blend with Chardonnay in Bourgogne Blanc. Grown throughout Italy, where it yields pleasant sparkling wine. Becoming popular in Germany, and grown throughout Austria, even being used to make botrytised Trockenbeerenauslese.

NEW WORLD Some is grown in Chile. Much of what is called Pinot Blanc in California is in fact another variety called Melon de Bourgogne (Loire's Muscadet).

PINOT GRIS

(Synonyms: Auvernat Gris, Grauer Burgunder, Malvoisie, Ruländer, Pinot Grigio, Tokay d'Alsace, Tokay-Pinot Gris)

MAINLY GROWN IN Alsace and northern Italy.

ALSO GROWN IN Austria, Germany, Hungary, Luxembourg, Oregon and Romania.

STYLE Many styles, from crisp, light and dry to fragrant and intense, to rich and honeyed.

WINES Can make a fine alternative to white burgundy, and great for matching with food.

ALSACE: Not only big, smoky, dry wines but also remarkably intense, oily and rich vendanges tardives (late-harvest) wines.

ITALY Known as Pinot Grigio, the grape makes wines that are lighter and spritzier than those produced elsewhere.

OTHER OLD WORLD REGIONS In the Loire, Pinot Gris is turned into pleasant rosés, while in the Valais region of Switzerland it gives rich, full wines. Germany makes juicy, spicily aromatic wines of low acidity, especially in Württemberg, Baden and Pfalz.

NEW WORLD Pinot Gris has never really caught on in the New World, although there are pockets of it in Mexico and the Willamette Valley in Oregon.

ROUSSANNE

(Synonyms: Bergeron, Rebelot, Picotin Blanc)

MAINLY GROWN IN Northern Rhône.

ALSO GROWN IN Australia, Languedoc-Roussillon, Savoie, Southern Rhône and Tuscany.

STYLE Roussanne has a haunting, hard-to-define, herbal bouquet and a good level of acidity, which helps it to age. But it can taste maderised between youth and maturity.

WINES Roussanne and Marsanne are the Laurel and Hardy of the wine world – Roussanne is delicate and Marsanne is fat. As they work so well as a double-act, the two grapes are invariably blended together.

RHÔNE In the northern Rhône, Roussanne and Marsanne produce white Hermitage, Crozes-Hermitage and St-Joseph, plus the sparkling wines of St-Péray. Roussanne is less widely grown than Marsanne, but it is the more elegant and aromatic of the two and ages much more gracefully. In the southern Rhône Roussanne is one of four grape varieties allowed in white and red Châteauneuf-du-Pape (Marsanne is not).

OTHER OLD WORLD Roussanne is successful in the Languedoc-Roussillon. Some Roussanne is also grown in Tuscany for the DOC wine Montecarlo.

SILVANER

(Synonyms: Grüner Silvaner, Franken, Johannisberger, Monterey Riesling, Sonoma Riesling, Sylvaner)

MAINLY GROWN IN Alsace, Germany, northern Italy and Switzerland.

ALSO GROWN IN Bulgaria and Hungary.

STYLE Light, soft wines with noticeable acidity and pleasant aromas; can lack body.

WINES Originated in Austria, where plantings have recently dwindled. Once the most planted variety in Germany, it has been overtaken by Müller-Thurgau.

ALSACE In France Sylvaner (it has a y instead of an i in Alsace) is virtually unknown

outside Alsace, where it is used to make pleasant but bland wines. It has more character in Alsace than in most regions.

GERMANY Despite the decline in new plantings, Silvaner is still widely grown in Germany and does especially well in Franken.

OTHER OLD WORLD Switzerland and northern Italy both make wines that are eminently drinkable but lack character.

NEW WORLD Silvaner used to be grown fairly widely in California, but has lost the race to Sauvignon Blanc and Chardonnay.

TREBBIANO

(Synonyms: Clairette Ronde, Muscadet Aigre, St-Emilion, Ugni Blanc, White Shiraz)

MAINLY GROWN IN France and Italy.

ALSO GROWN IN Australia, California, Eastern Europe, Greece, Mexico and Portugal.

STYLE Trebbiano makes neutral wines with little discernible aroma, which are high in acidity and short in length.

WINES Produces more of the world's wine than any other grape (although Airén is probably the most widely planted). Its wine is distilled into Cognac and Armagnac, and it goes into such blended Italian wines as Soave and Verdicchio.

FRANCE In France it is known as Ugni Blanc, but the grape's lack of character means that it is blended with more substantial varieties, or is distilled. About 80 per cent is made into Cognac or Armagnac, while the remainder goes into basic white wine such as Vin de Pays de Côtes de Gascogne.

ITALY In Italy, Trebbiano surfaces alongside other varieties in blends such as Frascati, Orvieto, Soave, and even finds its way into red Chianti.

NEW WORLD Grown in California and in Mexico – and used chiefly for distillation.

VIOGNIER

(Synonym: Vionnier)

MAINLY GROWN IN Northern Rhône.

ALSO GROWN IN Australia, California, Languedoc-Roussillon and Tuscany.

STYLE Hard to grow, but deep-yellow grapes produce a wine that is high in colour and alcohol, marked by a very particular, elusive aroma of peaches, pears, apricots and blossom.

WINES Now a fashionable variety.

NORTHERN RHÔNE Viognier gained its reputation by producing the extraordinarily intense, dry white wines from the tiny

vineyards of Condrieu. Unblended, Viognier tends to be heady and rich rather than bone-dry, but is also pricey, re-paying the vintners for all their hard work. Viognier is so entrenched in the northern Rhône that Côte-Rôtie, one of the region's most famous red wines, permits up to 20 per cent of the grape in its blend. Viognier is being planted elsewhere with increasing regularity.

NEW WORLD Australia has it and California adores it – Joseph Phelps in particular long having championed it. On the north Central Coast of America, Joseph Jensen of Calera makes a fine single-varietal example.

living with wine

STORING WINE

Some wines, such as top-quality claret, red burgundy, Sauternes, vintage champagne and vintage port, need time to mature; some wines, including most mid-quality wines, are unlikely to improve but will keep; and some wines, including most whites, rosés, simple low-priced wines of all colours and lighter reds, need to be drunk young.

But whatever the quality, it is important to look after wine while it is in your care. Some wine merchants offer storage facilities for a modest annual fee, which is useful for long-term maturation of top-quality wine but is impractical for the everyday stuff. If you intend to store wine, then you need only follow a few simple rules.

LOCATION AND TEMPERATURE Few people are lucky enough to have a wine cellar these days, so don't fret if you haven't got one. Any storage space that is dark, reasonably humid, free from vibrations and strong odours, and has an even temperature (that isn't too hot or too cold), can be transformed into your own personal "wine cellar". Places to avoid include kitchens or rooms near lift shafts or heavy machinery, as cooking smells are surprisingly pervasive and any vibrations can shake up sediment in the bottles. Studies, cloakrooms and the cupboard under the stairs are ideal places, as is the space under the bed provided your love life isn't too energetic.

Wine does like cool temperatures, but it isn't as fussy as some people think. Between 7°C and 13°C (45°F to 55°F) is OK; higher temperatures will cause wine to age more quickly and freezing temperatures can shatter bottles. Most important is consistency of temperature, and you should avoid excessive damp as it can corrode lead capsules, penetrate corks and cause labels to peel off.

STORAGE POSITION Once you have chosen a storage space, lay all your bottles on their sides to prevent the corks from drying out and shrinking. A wine-rack is ideal for this; many can be altered to fit the most unusual spaces. Ask at your local wine merchants or visit a DIY store for self-assembly models.

If you can't be bothered with a rack, use an empty wine box on its side. Fine wine in wooden cases should be left undisturbed – the bottles will already be lying flat and, should you wish to sell them, unopened cases fetch a better price than opened ones.

CELLAR BOOK It is well worth keeping a cellar book to record facts such as wine types and prices, when it was bought, what you've liked and what you haven't, what style goes well with particular foods, what needs drinking and what needs to be left. Cellar books are available to buy, but any notebook will do.

SERVING WINE

As any winemaker or wine merchant worth his corkscrew will tell you, there is only one hard and fast rule about serving or drinking wine: don't take it too seriously. Wine is surrounded by mystique, which can be part of its appeal, but worry about it slavishly and you won't enjoy it. The bottom line is that wine is a drink made from fermented grape juice, designed to give you pleasure. Bearing that in mind, here are a few tips to help you make the most of it.

CORKSCREWS The most reliable corkscrew is the "Screwpull™", a clever little tool that is almost infallible. However, in the event of a crumbling old cork or a new cork that refuses to budge, the two-pronged extractor known as the "Butler's Friend" is invaluable. It is worth having a reliable "Waiter's Knife" around too.

GLASSES There is a theory that different shapes of glasses should be used for different wines, both for visual effect and for getting the most enjoyment out of the wine. While this is fine if you have enough storage space, an arsenal of glasses isn't necessary. The only thing that matters is that your chosen glass has a stem, so that you can see the wine clearly and can hold the glass without the warmth of your hand affecting the wine's temperature. (That said, if you are ever offered some 1961 Château Latour with only a tooth-mug to hand, your duty is clear....)

One other crucial factor is that the wine glass must be clean. This may sound obvious, but "clean" in this instance means untainted by detergent or cupboard smells and well-polished. Get into the habit of rinsing your glasses thoroughly with hot water, and polish them dry afterwards with a clean, lint-free cloth.

Now to the fun part: pouring the wine. With the exception of champagne and sparkling wine, it's best to only half-fill the glass. This leaves room for you to swirl the wine around with abandon, showing off its colour and releasing its aroma or bouquet. You can always go back for a refill. Or two.

If you are hosting a party at home, fill your own glass first. This is sensible, not rude. It ensures that you, not your guests, get any stray specks of cork that are lurking in the top of the bottle and it allows you to taste the wine and check its condition – much less embarrassing than having a friend tell you that it's off.

SEQUENCE If you are having more than one wine with a meal, general rules to follow are: serve whites before reds, dry before sweet and light before full-bodied so that each wine has the chance to express itself. Serve older or more expensive wines first to enjoy them with a clear head.

TEMPERATURE Some books devote several pages to the "correct" temperatures for serving wine. Give us a break! All you need to remember is that red wine (apart from the very lightest, such as Beaujolais) is best served at room temperature to maximise its aroma, while white wine (sweet, dry and sparkling) is best either straight from a cool cellar or after an hour or so in the refrigerator. It's no more complicated than that.

If you want to chill a bottle of white wine or champagne quickly, chuck it in the freezer for half an hour (don't forget it, or it could explode), use a vini-cool™ sleeve (available at most wine merchants), or place it in an ice-bucket filled with a little ice and lots of water. The latter method might be messier and make the label soak off unless it is protected by a napkin, but it does lend a greater sense of occasion. If you simply want to keep (rather than make) a bottle cold, then a plastic or terracotta wine cooler will be effective for up to two hours – time enough for whatever *al fresco* devilry you might have in mind.

DECANTING There is no sense in uncorking red wine hours before drinking it; too little of it is exposed to the air to affect young wine, and the bouquet of old wine is apt to disappear. It is far better to decant the wine: this rids an older wine of its sediment and gives a younger wine a better chance to breathe. To warm a red wine in a hurry, decant it and then stand the decanter in warmish water.

Don't be put off by the so-called ritual of decanting and its associated paraphernalia. At its most studied, the process is conducted with a breathless hush in the solitude of the cellar using solid-silver funnels, candlesticks

and crystal decanters. However, it can be done just as effectively (if less dramatically) in the bedlam of the kitchen using a plastic funnel, lined with clean muslin or coffee filter paper, and a simple carafe. All that you need to do is pour your wine slowly through a filter into a waiting receptacle, thus trapping any gunk that lurks at the bottom of the bottle.

Fresh out of funnels? Don't panic: just pour the wine with a steady hand into the decanter or carafe, stopping once you see any sediment arrive in the neck of the bottle (a torch or candle comes in handy here). If you're fresh out of decanters and carafes, either use a glass jug or just pour the wine slowly into the glass straight from the bottle.

After regular use your decanter or carafe will become stained. To clean it, fill it with warm water, add a tablet of denture cleaner and leave it for 20 minutes or so before rinsing thoroughly. Alternatively, buy decanter "beads" for cleaning.

CHAMPAGNE AND SPARKLING WINES When is it appropriate to serve champagne? No-one has ever put it better than Madame Bollinger, who said: "I drink it when I'm happy and when I'm sad. Sometimes I drink it when I'm alone. When I have company I consider it obligatory. I trifle with it if I'm not hungry and drink it when I am. Otherwise I never touch it – unless I'm thirsty."

To open a bottle of champagne or sparkling wine, first remove the foil and the wire from around the cork, always keeping

your hand over the cork. Hold the bottle at a 45-degree slant, with the base in your strong hand and the cork in the other. Twist the bottle while holding the cork steady (if you do it the other way around, you risk shearing the cork). Ease the cork out slowly, covering it with the palm of your hand or a tea-towel at all times. The carbon dioxide in the bottle, combined with your gentle external encouragement, should result in the cork emerging, not with a loud bang, but with a satisfied and seductive sigh... and you won't risk putting someone's eye out.

Unless you have no choice, don't serve champagne and sparkling wine in flat "saucers" or *coupés*. Such glasses might well have been modelled on Marie-Antoinette's breasts and, yes, they are perfect for suggestive slurps with a showgirl or two, but they allow the precious bubbles to escape much too easily. It is far better to use the tall glasses known as "flutes", which help retain the wine's sparkle.

In the unlikely and humiliating event that you cannot finish a bottle of champagne, a champagne-stopper will keep the bubbles fresh for up to 36 hours. However, a metal teaspoon placed handle-down in the neck of the bottle is just as effective and a lot cheaper (goodness knows how it works – it just does).

PORT Vintage port must be decanted since it is apt to throw a large sediment; once decanted, it should be drunk within two or three days to enjoy its freshness. Other types of port, particularly tawny, don't need to be decanted and will remain drinkable for far longer than a vintage port.

For some reason, it is traditional to pass the port to the left at the dining table. This doesn't make it taste any better, nor does it stop the Tower of London from falling down. It does mean, however, that at a dinner for 10, the person gasping for a refill immediately to your right might die of thirst before the decanter can complete a circuit of the table (by which time it will probably be empty anyway). Such a tradition serves no purpose other than to make inexperienced wine-drinkers feel inadequate and excluded, so ignore it. Just share and enjoy.

TASTING WINE

LOOKING AT WINE Fill no more than a quarter of your glass and look at the wine, preferably against a white background (a table cloth of sheet of paper will do). The wine should be clear and bright without any cloudiness or haziness. White wine ranges in colour from watery pale to rich gold, while red runs from rosy pink to opaque black. Although grape varieties, regions of origin and methods of production all combine to determine a wine's colour, generally speaking red wine turns paler and less rich in colour as it ages (often displaying hints of orange and brown at the rim of the glass), while white wine grows darker.

SMELLING WINE Holding the stem, swirl the glass around to release the bouquet. Put your nose to the glass and take a good sniff. First impressions are the most reliable. The wine should smell clean and fresh, and will almost certainly remind you of something that has nothing to do with wine. Cabernet Sauvignon, for example, often smells of blackcurrants, Gewürztraminer of lychees. Almost anything that might be wrong with a wine can be detected on the nose by odours of mustiness, vinegar or sulphur.

TASTING WINE Take a sip of the wine, then pucker your lips and draw air between them as you hold the wine in your mouth (early attempts invariably lead to copious dribbling, but who cares?). Roll the liquid around every part of your mouth, then spit into the nearest spittoon, or swallow.

Is the wine sweet or dry, light or full-bodied? Is it full of harsh tannins (as some young reds are) or bursting with generous fruit? Familiar tastes will soon spring to mind: Sauvignon Blanc reminds many people of gooseberries, Chardonnay of butter, vanilla or tropical fruit; Syrah of black pepper and spice, and so on. Try to commit these associations to memory.

A fine wine should have good length, meaning that its taste should linger after you have swallowed it or spat it out. The overall impression should be one of balance, which means that all the wine's components – its acidity, alcohol, fruit and tannin – have combined in one harmonious whole.

Just remember, each time you uncork a bottle, someone, somewhere, has gone to a lot of trouble to make this wine, but that doesn't mean you need to analyse its every nuance. The winemaker would far rather you just sat down and enjoyed the fruits of his or her labour.

wine with food

WINE AND FOOD DIRECTORY

It's easy to get the impression that some wine and food pairings are inscribed in tablets of stone and others are a criminal offence. But tastes differ, and while you should not ignore the experiences of others, it is fun to experiment. Any number of pairings can be successful; you need only ensure that your chosen wine complements your dish.

The weight (concentration of flavour, alcohol content and amount of oak and tannin) of the wine is more important than its colour. For example, a simple light dish such as grilled salmon needs a light wine with acidity and elegance, possibly a Chablis or a Pinot Noir from California; whereas a rich, heavy stew is best matched with a big, full-bodied wine (red or white) – a Syrah from the Rhône perhaps, or an oak-aged Chardonnay.

Remember to think about sauces and secondary ingredients in the dish – these can dramatically change or add to the flavour profile and hence influence the choice of wine.

It is widely believed that dessert wines should only be served with pudding; well, as anyone who has had a glass of Sauternes with a stinky blue cheese such as Roquefort will tell you, that simply ain't so. But for what it is worth, there follows a selection of tried and tested pairings.

BARBECUES (red meat): Syrah/Shiraz, Zinfandel. (*See also* kebabs).
BEEF Almost any red wine with good weight, especially Bordeaux, burgundy, Rioja, or the wine used in the sauce.
BISCUITS Madeira, medium to sweet sherry, port, Italian vin santo, dry Marsala.
BURGERS Fruity, medium-bodied reds from Chile, Australia or southern France.
BOUILLABAISSE Dry whites, especially Loire.
CANAPÉS Sparkling wine, chilled *fino* or *manzanilla* sherry, any light dry white wine.
CAVIAR Champagne, of course.
CASSEROLES Hearty, spicy reds such as Rioja (oak-aged *crianza* or *reserva* are best), Rhône wines, Australian Shiraz or Cabernet Sauvignon, and even big oak-aged Chardonnays from Burgundy or California.
CASSOULET Syrah, Rioja.
CHEESE *Brie* White burgundy, Beaujolais. *Camembert* Merlot (reds tend to clash with, or be blown away by, unpasteurised cheeses, so try unoaked Chardonnay with these). *Goat's* Sauvignon Blanc. *Gruyère* Red burgundy. *Münster* Alsace Gewurztraminer (sweeter styles are better). *Roquefort* Sauternes, French Liqueur Muscats, Tokáji. *Stilton* Port, dry *oloroso* sherry.
CHICKEN *Coq au Vin* Red burgundy, southern French red.

Grilled Côtes du Rhône, Beaujolais, Chianti, and most dry whites.

Roast Pinot Noir, Chardonnay, Chianti.

CHILLI CON CARNE Zinfandel (if the dish is very hot, the chilli and tannins will clash, so try oak-free Cabernets, or even Loire red).

CHINESE FOOD Gewürztraminer, Pinot Gris, Alsace Muscat.

CHOCOLATE Black Muscat, Orange Muscat, sweet Madeira or Marsala.

CHOUCROUTE Any dry wines from Alsace.

COLD MEATS Barbera, claret, Beaujolais.

CRAB Chardonnay, dry white Bordeaux, dry Loire.

CURRY Lager is ideal (best are good-quality Germanic/Eastern European bottled styles with noticeable malt and hop characters). Otherwise go for fruity unoaked white wines with a touch of sweetness, such as Chardonnay, or fruity dry(ish) rosés. German *Spätlese* can work with chicken- or fish-based dishes.

CUSTARDS Sweet Loire or Sauternes.

DUCK *Grilled* Chilean Merlot or Cabernet Sauvignon is ideal.

Roast Claret, Rioja, Beaujolais-Villages such as Fleurie or Morgon

In rich sauces Serve southern Italian reds or sweetish Loire whites with rich, sweet and fruity sauces, or unoaked Pinotage from South Africa with spicy sauces.

FISH *Grilled* Sauvignon Blanc, Riesling, young modern-style white Rioja, dry rosés.

In rich sauces Riesling, white burgundy, dry white Bordeaux.

and chips English dry whites, Valpolicella

Pâté Pinot Blanc, Riesling.

FOIE GRAS *Pâté* Sauternes, Vouvray, *demi-sec* champagne.

Grilled Viognier, Chardonnay, Pinot Noir.

FRUIT: *Poached pears* Moscato d'Asti

Tart Sauternes, German Auslese, Muscat de Beaumes-de-Venise, Gewürztraminer.

Strawberries and cream Sauternes, Muscat de Beaumes-de-Venise, German *Beerenauslese*, sweet Loire.

GOOSE Rioja, northern Rhônes, German *Spätlese* (Pfalz or Baden rather than Mosel).

GROUSE Zinfandel, Côtes du Rhône.

HAM Pinot Noir, white burgundy, Beaujolais. For Parma/Serrano types try Valpolicella Classico or Penedès, Navarra from Spain.

JAPANESE FOOD Most dry whites.

JUGGED HARE Meaty reds based on Syrah, Barolo, Rioja (*reserva*).

KEBABS *Fish* Riesling, Verdicchio, light Pinot Noir.

White meat Marsanne, Pinot Noir.

Red meat Syrah, southern French red.

Vegetable Dry rosé, southern Italian reds.

LAMB *Grilled* Most reds, especially Barolo, claret, Chilean or South African Merlot and Cabernet Sauvignon, Zinfandel, Rioja (*reserva*), Syrah.

Roast Claret, California Cabernet Sauvignon, Australian Shiraz, Rhône reds.

LOBSTER White Bordeaux, Chardonnay, Alsace Pinot Gris.

MOUSSAKA Greek reds, Rioja.

NUTS Madeira, tawny port, *fino* sherry.

OLIVES Dry sherry.

ONION TART Alsace Riesling or Sylvaner.

OYSTERS Muscadet, dry white Bordeaux, Chablis, Sancerre.

PACIFIC RIM Gewürztraminer, Riesling, Pinot Gris.

PASTA *With fish sauce* Pinot Grigio, Soave. *With meat sauce* Most reds, especially Chianti, Valpolicella, Rioja, Zinfandel. *With pesto* Lighter Chardonnays, Sauvignon Blanc, Chianti.

PHEASANT Claret, red burgundy, northern Rhône reds.

PIGEON Rioja (*crianza* or *reserva*), claret.

PIZZA Chianti, Rioja. Simple tomato-based pizza goes well with fresh, dry whites.

PORK *Loin* Pinot Noir, Australian Semillon. *Roast* Côtes du Rhône, Portuguese red.

QUICHE Beaujolais, Alsace Pinot Noir.

RABBIT Red burgundy, Chianti, robust southern French reds.

RISOTTO Barbera, full-flavoured dry whites.

SALADS Riesling, Beaujolais (depending on what is in it and what dressing is used).

SALMON *Grilled* California Pinot Noir, white burgundy, dry rosé. *Hollandaise* Dry white Bordeaux, Chardonnay. *Poached* Soave, unoaked Chardonnay, Frascati, dry German Riesling Kabinett (aged). *Smoked* Champagne, Alsace Riesling or light dry Gewurztraminer, Pinot Grigio, white Rhône, white burgundy.

SAUSAGES Spicy, oaky reds – Italian or Spanish, Syrah/Shiraz, spicy Alsace whites.

SCALLOPS Dry white Bordeaux, Riesling, lighter Chardonnays.

SEAFOOD Chablis, any dry Loire, dry-ish German, dry Vinho Verde, Albariño.

SOUP Dry sherry.

STEAK California Cabernet, Australian Shiraz, northern Rhône reds.

THAI FOOD Gewürztraminer, Australian Verdelho.

TUNA Pinot Noir, Riesling, Beaujolais.

TURKEY Gewürztraminer (for fresh, full-flavoured birds), Sauvignon Blanc, Chardonnay, Beaujolais.

VEAL *Roast* White burgundy, Pinot Noir, Beaujolais, Côtes du Rhône. *With mushrooms* Red burgundy. *In light sauce* White burgundy. *In cream sauce* Sauvignon Blanc, Riesling.

VEGETABLE-BASED DISHES Côtes du Rhône, Barbera, Spanish red.

VENISON Grenache, Rioja, Malbec.

WILD BOAR As for Jugged Hare, plus Provence or Languedoc red, Portuguese red.

WINE IN RESTAURANTS

THE WINE LIST A well-chosen wine can mask the deficiencies of a poor meal and highlight the qualities of a great one, so it is important to take plenty of time to study a wine list before making your choice. The list might be arranged by wine colour, wine region or by country, vintage or price.

Some restaurants state that if a certain vintage is unavailable they will substitute it with a subsequent one. This is acceptable for some wines – such as a Muscadet, or an everyday Australian Chardonnay – but not for finer wines; for example, you wouldn't want a 1983 vintage claret to be replaced with one from 1984.

Don't forget that a good restaurant should have decent house wines available by the glass as well as by the bottle. Don't be shy about ordering such wines. If in doubt, ask the *sommelier* (wine waiter) to tell you more about them.

Whatever dining out experience you have in mind, the following points should help you to navigate your way through the wine list.

* When the bottle is brought to you, make sure it is exactly what you ordered (*château*, vintage etc).

* Check that the wine's temperature is acceptable. If a white is too warm, ask for an ice bucket; if a red is too cool, ask for it to be left to warm for 15 minutes or so before pouring.

* Whatever you have ordered should be opened at the table in front of you – unless it is house wine, which might be brought in a carafe.

* If red wine is to be decanted, ask that this be done at your table. No serious *sommelier* would object to this (they love the opportunity to show off).

* Some *sommeliers* sniff the cork once it is removed from the bottle or invite the customer to do so; this is an affectation and will tell you nothing about the condition of the wine.

* You should always be invited to taste the wine (although some restaurants do not ask diners to taste their house wines). Don't be flustered; take your time. Almost everything that could be wrong with a wine can be detected by looking at it in the glass (it should be bright and clear, whatever the colour) and by smelling its aroma (which, if something is amiss, will smell musty, damp or downright horrible). Look at it, smell it, taste it – and if you think anything is wrong with it, don't hesitate to say so.

* Don't be hurried into tasting a wine that follows another. If you're in the middle of a plate of smoked salmon and a glass of Pouilly-Fumé when the wine waiter asks you to taste the red burgundy you ordered for the next course,

ask him to return when you have finished. It is important not to mix up wines and courses; the burgundy would taste grim, and it deserves a more sympathetic first encounter.

* If you don't see a wine that you want on the wine list, ask for it. The restaurant may well have what you desire, but in too small a quantity to merit putting it on the wine list. Similarly, some enlightened establishments will, if asked, allow customers to purchase some of their popular wines by the glass, especially dessert wines, because few people want to buy a whole bottle.

* If in doubt about your choice, ask the wine waiter for his or her advice. If the restaurant does not have a *sommelier* or a waiter who is reasonably versed in wine, trust your instincts, play it safe and have the courage of your convictions.

* Some restaurants allow customers to bring in their own wine, which the waiter will open and serve. There is often a charge for this (known as corkage), which is reasonable considering that you are depriving the establishment of one of its main sources of profit. Ask how much the charge is in advance; in some cases you might feel that it would be cheaper or more diplomatic to have something from the restaurant's own wine list.

Unlicensed restaurants often advertise the fact that you can bring your own bottle of wine (known as BYOB), in which case there is rarely a charge, or if there is it is a nominal one.

wine glossary

GETTING TO GRIPS WITH WINESPEAK

Whether it appears on wine labels or is being bandied around at dinner parties, restaurants and tastings, the language of wine can be confusing. The following terms will help you navigate your way through the previously uncharted shelves of your local wine merchant and will enable you to hold your head high at any gathering of wine-lovers.

ACID/ACIDITY Acids, primarily citric, malic and tartaric, occur naturally in wine and, in the proper proportion, are essential ingredients, giving the wine character and helping it age. As a rule, cool regions produce wines that are high in acidity, while warm regions produce wines that are low in acidity.

ADDITIVES Winemakers are allowed to use over 40 additives (which differ from region to region) to control oxidisation and bacterial damage, and to ensure that the wine is cleared of impurities. For example, ammonium sulphatrains are used to encourage yeasts to grow during production, while ascorbic acid, citric acid, potassium metabosulphate and sulphur dioxide (the most commonly used additive, and the only one permitted in organic wines) might be employed as preservatives. Although sugar is forbidden as a sweetener, it is used as an additive in some regions (legally) to raise alcohol levels, and gum arabic can be used to clear wine of iron or copper traces. Several other substances are also used during fining (*see* Fining).

ALCOHOL The alcohol present in wine, ranging from about 6.5 to 14 per cent, is ethyl alcohol (C_2H_5OH), also known as ethanol, the result of the interaction of yeasts with grape sugar during fermentation.

APPELLATION CONTRÔLÉE (AC or AOC, French) Part of French law that guarantees that a wine comes from where the label says it does, that it is made from specific grapes and that it is produced in a certain way. (*See also* page seven.)

ARMAGNAC A region in France, southeast of Bordeaux, which produces a fine brandy of the same name.

AROMA The smell of a wine. As the wine matures and takes on more complex characteristics, the term can change to bouquet. If this seems like splitting hairs, you can always refer to the wine's smell – everyone will know what you mean and only a wine-snob would correct you (*see* Nose).

BALANCE Good balance refers to a wine in which the acids, tannins, alcohol, fruit and flavour are all in pleasing proportions.

BARRIQUE (French) The regular Bordeaux oak barrel of 225 litres.

BEREICH (German) Wine-producing district.

BIANCO (Italian) White.

BLANC (French) White.

BLANC DE BLANCS (French) A white wine made exclusively from white grapes.

BLANC DE NOIRS (French) A white wine made exclusively from red grapes (usually used to refer to champagnes made solely from Pinot Noir).

BLANCO (Spanish) White.

BLENDING A wine can be a blend of different varieties, different vintages, different areas and even different barrels. The blender's skill lies in getting the blend right year after year.

BLIND TASTING A tasting of wines where all clues as to the wines' identities – including the labels and shapes of the bottles – are obscured from the tasters. (Not to be confused with blind drunk.)

BLUSH WINE *See* Rosé.

BODEGA (Spanish) Winery, wine company or wine cellar; also refers to an above-ground cellar and to a restaurant's wine cellar. Called *adega* in Galicia.

BODY Term used to describe the weight and the structure of a wine. Supermodels aren't the only things that need a good body.

BOTRYTIS CINEREA *See* Noble rot.

BOTTLE The standard wine bottle usually holds 75cl. Larger bottles, such as litres and magnums, are also often seen, and the rule of thumb is that the larger the bottle, the more slowly the wine within it will mature (and the longer it will keep) due to the ratio of wine to oxygen in the bottle. Other bottle sizes are available, although they become rarer the further down the list you go:

Quarter bottle (Champagne) 20cl.

Half bottle 37.5cl.

"Imp" [Imperial] 50cl.

Bottle 75cl.

Litre 100cl.

Magnum Equivalent to two 75cl bottles.

Marie-Jeanne (Bordeaux) Equivalent to three 75cl bottles.

Double Magnum Equivalent to four 75cl bottles.

Jeroboam (Champagne) Equivalent to four 75cl bottles.

Jeroboam (Bordeaux) Equivalent to six 75cl bottles.

Rehoboam (Champagne) Equivalent to six 75cl bottles.

Impériale (Bordeaux) Equivalent to eight 75cl bottles.

Methuselah (Champagne) Equivalent to eight 75cl bottles.

Salmanazar (Champagne) Equivalent to 12 75cl bottles.

Balthazar (Champagne) Equivalent to 16 75cl bottles.

Nebuchadnezzar (Champagne) Equivalent to 20 75cl bottles.

BOTTLE STINK The stale whiff – usually of bad eggs, that can hit the drinker as a bottle of wine is opened. It usually disappears within seconds, and it doesn't necessarily mean anything is wrong with the wine.

BOUQUET The scent of a wine that develops as it ages and matures. (*See also* Nose and Aroma.)

BRANDY A spirit distilled from wine, the most famous of which are Cognac, Armagnac and *marc*. (*See also* Eau-de-vie.)

BULK PROCESS See *Cuve close*.

BRUT The term given to a dry champagne and to a once alarmingly popular aftershave.

BUTTERY Term used to describe the beguiling smell of butter, often found in white wines, particularly Chardonnay.

CANTINA (Italian) Winery or cellar.

CAPSULE Covering, usually made of lead or plastic, that protects the top of the cork in the neck of a wine bottle. Several producers, especially in the New World, are beginning to dispense with capsules.

CARAFE Poor man's decanter – used for the same purpose, but without a stopper.

CARBONIC MACERATION Whole bunches of grapes ferment inside their skins under a blanket of CO_2. The juice is gently squeezed out by the weight of the grapes to make light, fruity wines.

CAVE (French) Cellar.

CELLAR BOOK A book in which wine-lovers record comments on the wines that enter and leave their cellars (or cupboards under the stairs).

CEPA (Spanish/Portuguese) Term for grape variety.

CEPAGE (French) Term for grape variety.

CHAI (French) Building, usually above ground, in which wine is stored to mature.

CHAMBRER (French) To allow a wine gradually to reach room temperature before drinking.

CHARMAT PROCESS See *Cuve close*.

CHÂTEAU (French) Term given to a wine-growing property (which doesn't necessarily include a castle or fine building).

CLARET Term given to the red wines of Bordeaux; a corruption of the French word *clairet*, meaning light red wine.

CLASSED GROWTHS See *Cru classé*.

CLIMAT (French) Burgundian term for a particular vineyard.

CLOS (French) An enclosed vineyard, used particularly in Alsace and Burgundy.

COGNAC A town in western France, in and around which the world's most celebrated brandy of the same name is produced.

COLHEITA (Portuguese) Vintage. Also a term used for wood-matured, single-vintage ports.

CORK The bung used to stopper wine bottles. Most corks are still made from the outer bark of the cork oak (*Quercus suber*), found mainly in Portugal. However, producers continue to experiment with substitutes, and synthetic corks are being seen much more frequently.

CORKAGE Nothing to do with corked, but the term given to the charge levied by a restaurant on wine brought in by customers to consume with a meal.

CORKED A condition often heralded by a damp, musty odour, whereby the cork of a bottle is diseased or weevil-ridden, thus tainting the taste and smell of the wine. Wines of any quality can be corked. The term is often erroneously used to describe wine that is "off" and it does not refer to any harmless fragments of cork that might remain in a glass or bottle.

COSECHA (Spanish) Vintage or harvest.

CÔTE (French) A slope or hillside, in this instance covered with vineyards.

CRADLE A basket in which a bottle of undecanted red wine, usually burgundy, is sometimes served in restaurants. It might look fancy, but it is hopelessly impractical, because each time the wine is poured and set down again, the sediment within the bottle is churned about.

CRÉMANT (French) Literally "creaming", the term refers to sparkling wines and champagnes which are fizzier than *pétillant* but not as fizzy as *mousseux*.

CRU (French) A growth or vineyard.

CRU CLASSÉ (French) A term which translates into English as "classed growth". In 1855, 61 red wines of the Médoc (including one from Graves: Château Haut-Brion) were classified as *cru classé*, which were divided into five ranks determined by price (and therefore, in theory, quality), ranging from *premier cru* (first growth) down to *cinquième cru* (fifth growth). At the same time, the sweet white wines of Sauternes were divided into three categories: *premier grand cru*, *premier cru* and *deuxième cru*, or first great growth, first growth and second growth. Although now hopelessly outdated, these classifications do still denote a lot of prestige to a property and its wines. Only one wine, Château Mouton-Rothschild, has ever changed category; after much lobbying by its owner, Baron Philippe de Rothschild, it was promoted from *deuxième cru* to *premier cru* in 1973.

In 1955, also in Bordeaux, the wines of St-Emilion were similarly classified into three ranks (*premier grand cru classé*, *grand cru classé* and *grand cru*), while *grand cru classé* (without subdivisions) has also been used since 1953 for red wines of Graves and, since 1959, for white wines of that area.

CRU BOURGEOIS (French) The term given to Médoc wines categorised just below those of *cru classé* status.

CUVE CLOSE (French) Process of producing sparkling wine in stainless-steel tanks, and thus more cheaply and in greater bulk than by the *méthode traditionelle*. *Cuve close* is also known as the bulk, or Charmat, process, named after Eugène Charmat, the Frenchman who developed it in the early 1900s.

CUVÉE (French) A blended wine or a special selection.

DECANTER Clear glass receptacle with a stopper, usually of elegant design, into which red wine or port is poured in order to allow it to breathe or to separate it from its sediment. (*See also* Carafe.)

DEMI-SEC (French) Semi-sweet.

DESSERT WINE Term given to sweet wines which might owe their intensity either to having been fortified or to having been attacked by noble rot. Traditionally drunk at the end of a meal with pudding, dessert wines are equally delicious with strong cheeses or rich pâtés. (*See also* Noble rot.)

DOLCE (Italian) Sweet.

DOMAINE (French) Property or estate.

DOUX (French) Sweet.

DULCE (Spanish) Sweet.

EAU-DE-VIE (French) Literally "water of life", a general term for an unsweetened, colourless spirit distilled from fermented natural fruit juice, the most common of which is brandy, made from grapes. Of other fruit spirits, Normandy's Calvados, made from apples, is perhaps the best known, while Alsace is famous for its Mirabelle (from yellow plums), Quetsch (from blue plums), Kirsch (from cherries), Framboise (from raspberries), Fraise (from strawberries) and Poire William (from pears).

EDELFÄULE (German) Noble rot.

EN PRIMEUR (French) The system whereby each spring, following the vintage, the châteaux of Bordeaux reveal the opening prices of their new wines. Customers pay in advance for these wines through wine merchants and take delivery of them after bottling some 18 months later. This method ensures that customers get the wines that they want, and almost always at the most advantageous prices. Prices rarely fall after the opening offer.

FERMENTATION The natural process whereby grape juice turns into wine. Sugars are converted by yeast enzymes into alcohol and carbon dioxide.

FINING A process in which minuscule particles that might cloud a wine or adversely affect its taste are removed. This is done by adding an agent to the wine which absorbs such particles and sinks to the bottom, after which the sediment is removed and the wine is filtered and bottled. The most frequently used materials include egg whites, dried ox blood, gelatin, isinglass (a form of gelatin made from the air bladders of fish) charcoal, clay (usually bentonite), silica gel or powdered milk protein (known as casein). Mmm, nice… (*see* Additives).

FLOR Yeasts that grow on the top of *fino* and *manzanilla* sherries, protecting them from oxidisation and giving them a distinctive aroma and taste.

FORTIFIED WINE A wine such as port, sherry, Madeira or *Vin Doux Naturel*, to which brandy or neutral spirit has been added, either to arrest its fermentation before all the sugar is turned into alcohol (thus preserving its sweetness) or simply to strengthen it.

FRIZZANTE (Italian) Semi-sparkling.

GRAND CRU (French) Term used for top-quality wines in Alsace, Bordeaux, Burgundy and champagne. (*See also* Cru classé.)

GRAPPA (Italian) See *Marc*.

HALBTROCKEN (German) Medium dry.

HOCK Properly, the word given to wines made in and around the town of Hochheim on the River Main in Germany, but more frequently an English term applied to all white Rhine wines. Such wines are recognisable by their brown bottles, as opposed to Moselle wines which come in green bottles.

HORIZONTAL TASTING Nothing to do with laying down or the result of over-imbibing, but simply a tasting of different wines from a single vintage. (*See also* Vertical tasting.)

JAHRGANG (German) Vintage.

JUG WINE General term used (mostly in the US) for inexpensive wine in large bottles.

KELLER (German) Cellar.

LABELS Like this book, a wine label should tell you everything you need to know about a wine. New World wine labels sometimes seem to tell you too much, such as the date and time of the harvest, the amount of egg whites used to fine the liquid and the name of the bottling-line manager's wife, while European wine labels prefer to tell you the bare minimum. Most wine laws insist that the labels reveal the following:

- The wine's name
- The size of the bottle
- The wine's vintage, if applicable
- The wine's alcoholic strength
- The producer's (or the shipper's) name and address
- The wine's quality level
- Where the wine was bottled
- What region the wine is from
- Some labels also include the grape variety

Wines imported into the US, or exported from there, are also obliged to display a government health warning concerning the hazards of drinking wine. (Huh!)

LANDWEIN (German) A level of quality wine just above simple table wine, equivalent to the French *vin de pays*.

LATE HARVEST Very ripe grapes picked late when their sweetness is most concentrated. (*See also Vendange tardive*.)

LAYING DOWN The practice of storing

mid- to top-quality red wines, ports, champagnes and white wines from their purchase when young until they are ready to drink in their maturity. Depending on the wine in question, this period can be anything from a number of months to several decades.

LEGS A term often bandied around tastings is that a given wine in the glass "has good legs". This doesn't mean that it could pass muster in a chorus line, but that tears of glycerine can be detected falling down the inside rim of the glass after it has been swirled about, usually indicating that the wine is young and/or high in alcohol and invariably rich in flavour.

MADERISED A condition whereby a white wine is close to being oxidised, often characterised by a deep orange hue and a taste not dissimilar to sherry or Madeira.

MARC (French) A rough brandy made from the discarded skins, pips and stalks of crushed grapes. The Italian and Californian equivalent is known as *grappa*.

MERITAGE Term used in the US to describe red and white blends that specifically use the Rhône or Bordeaux grape varieties.

MÉTHODE TRADITIONELLE The method (known in Champagne as *méthode champenoise*), involving a secondary fermentation in bottle, by which champagne and top-quality sparkling wines are made. Only wine made in Champagne in this manner may be called champagne, so producers from outside the region use this term to distinguish their product from lesser-quality sparkling wine made by other methods such as *cuve close*.

MIS(E) EN BOUTEILLE(S) AU CHÂTEAU
(French) The wine was bottled at the property at which it was made.

MOELLEUX (French) Sweet.

MOUSSE (French) The satisfying froth that fizzes in a glass of champagne or sparkling wine as it is poured, savoured and drunk.

MOUSSEUX (French) Sparkling.

MULLED WINE A warming drink that never fails to hit the spot on a cold winter's day. The simplest of all recipes is to mix a bottle of basic red wine with half as much water, a small glass of brandy, two or three lumps of sugar, a pinch or two of nutmeg and a little cinnamon. Heat but don't boil, and garnish each glass with a slice of lemon.

NÉGOCIANT (French) Wine merchant, shipper or grower who buys wine or grapes in bulk from several sources before vinifying and or bottling the wine himself.

NOBLE ROT Not the rubbish heard spoken at smart wine tastings, but the name given to Botrytis cinerea, known as *pourriture noble* in France or *edelfäule* in Germany. Basically, botrytis is a mould that is encouraged to attack certain grapes (most successfully Sauvignon Blanc, Sémillon, Chenin Blanc and Gewürztraminer in France and Riesling in Germany) prior to harvesting, making them shrivel and rot, and thus concentrating their sugars and flavours. Nobly rotten or "botrytised" grapes are used to make dessert wines that are high in alcohol and richness of flavour.

NON-VINTAGE (NV) Term applied to any wine that is a blend of two or more vintages, but especially relevant to port or champagne.

NOSE The overall "sense" given off by a wine on being smelled. It is not just the wine's scent; the nose also conveys information about the wine's well-being. Both aroma and bouquet are encompassed by the term, which has nothing whatever to do with the shiny red proboscis sported by your wine merchant.

OAK A lot of wines are aged in oak barrels, a fact that can often be detected on the nose, and is typified by aromas of vanilla or cedar. Such a wine might be said to be "oaky".

OENOPHILE (also enophile) Wine-lover.

ORGANIC The regulations governing the use of the term "organic" are constantly changing, and the term itself can also be misleading. It generally means that the grapes have been organically grown (ie without the use of synthetic fertilizers and pesticides). Sulphur dioxide may legally be used during an organic wine's production. The word "organic" does not mean that the wine has not come into contact with non-organic materials during the fining, storing, ageing or even bottling stages.

OXIDISED Deterioration owing to the wine's contact with too much air for too long. (*See also* Maderised.)

PERLANT (French) A wine with the very gentlest of sparkles in it, synonymous with "spritzy".

PERLWEIN (German) A type of semi-sparkling wine, usually of low quality.

PÉTILLANT (French) Slightly sparkling.

PHYLLOXERA A louse which attacks the roots of vines with disastrous results. Nearly all European varieties are susceptible; the continents's vineyards were devastated in the 1860s and 1870s. Consequently, grapevines are now invariably grafted onto more resistant American root-stocks. Some pockets of resistance are found, mainly in Chile (owing to its sandy soil) and occasionally in parts of Europe.

POURRITURE NOBLE (French) *See* Noble rot.

PUNT The indentation at the bottom of a bottle. It not only catches any sediment there might be in the wine, but it also strengthens the bottle.

QUINTA (Portuguese) Wine-growing estate or property.

RÉCOLTE (French) Crop or vintage.

ROSADO (Spanish) Rosé.

ROSATO (Italian) Rosé.

ROSÉ A pink wine (known as blush wine in America) made from red grapes in the same manner as red wine, except that the skins of the grapes are removed sooner, leaving a more delicate colour and a lighter style of wine. A few wines, notably pink champagnes, are made by adding red wine to white wine.

ROSSO (Italian) Red.

ROUGE (French) Red.

SEC (French) Dry.

SECCO (Italian) Dry.

SECO (Spanish/Portuguese) Dry.

SEDIMENT The dregs – a good indication of a wine's age – that should remain in the bottom of a bottle after decanting. If you are doing your own decanting, it is well worth keeping the deposit for cooking or marinading.

SEKT (German) Sparkling wine.

SÉLECTION DES GRAINS NOBLE Wine made from late-picked, over-ripe grapes, which is similar to *vendange tardive*, or late-harvested, wine, but with a higher sugar content (*see also Vendange tardive*).

SINGLE VARIETAL *See* Varietal.

SOLERA Perpetual system of blending used in the production of sherry and Madeira, whereby old wines are continuously mixed with new ones.

SOMMELIER A wine waiter.

SPARKLING WINE General term given to any fizzy wine. More specifically, it refers to all fizzy wines, however grand or humble and made by whatever method, that come from outside Champagne.

SPITTOON Any receptacle, from a silver bowl to a wooden box filled with sawdust, used to collect the spat-out samples of wines at tastings.

SPRITZER A refreshing drink made from white wine and soda or sparkling mineral water, usually served with ice.

SPRITZY *See Perlant.*

SPUMANTE (Italian) Sparkling.

SUR LIE Wines bottled directly after fermentation on their lees or sediment, which hence have greater depth of flavour.

TAFELWEIN (German) Table wine.

TANNIN The mouth-puckering taste found in some red wines, usually young ones, which originates from grape skins and stalks combined with the oak barrels in which the wine has been aged. Such a wine might be said to be tannic. A similar sensation might be experienced after drinking poorly made or long-brewed teas.

TARTRATES Crystals of potassium bitartrate which sometimes appear in cask or bottle owing to the natural presence of tartaric acid. They are harmless.

TASTEVIN (French) A small silver tasting cup, most common in Burgundy.

TERROIR (French) At its simplest, the word means "soil", but winemakers use it to refer to the differing types of soil, climate, drainage and position of a vineyard.

TINTO (Spanish/Portuguese) Red.

TROCKEN (German) Dry.

ULLAGE The amount of air in a bottle or barrel between the top of the wine and the bottom of the cork or bung. If the level of liquid is below the top of the bottle's shoulder, the wine is said to be "ullaged".

VARIETAL A wine named after the grape (or its major constituent grape) from which it is made.

VENDANGE (French) The harvest or vintage.

VENDANGE TARDIVE (French) Late harvest (see also Sélection des grains noble).

VENDEMMIA (Italian) The harvest or vintage.

VENDIMIA (Spanish) The harvest or vintage.

VERMOUTH A fortified white wine flavoured with herbs and spices.

VERTICAL TASTING Tasting of the same wine from different vintages (see Horizontal tasting).

VIGNERON (French) Vine grower.

VIN DE PAYS (French) Country wine of a level higher than table wine.

VIN DE TABLE (French) Table wine.

VIN DOUX NATUREL (VDN) (French) A fortified sweet wine.

VIN ORDINAIRE (French) Basic wine not subject to any regulations.

VINIFICATION The process of making wine.

VINO DA TAVOLA (Italian) Table wine.

VINO DE MESA (Spanish) Table wine.

VINTAGE The harvest, and the term given to a wine of a particular year as stated on the label.

VITICULTURE The cultivation of grapes.

WEIGHT Term given to the concentration of flavour, alcohol content and amount of oak and tannin of a wine.

hangover cures

Nobody's perfect. Even the most serious wine drinker will, at some time or other, suffer from a rebellious liver and an unreceptive or jaded palate – otherwise known as a hangover.

The best way to fight this condition, which is caused chiefly by dehydration and low blood-sugar levels, is to drink plenty of water and to avoid black coffee (caffeine is a diuretic, so you'll be losing valuable fluids). Vitamins B and C are important too.

But if you get out of bed late in the day and all else fails, you'll find that life can look a little rosier after the hair of the dog that bit you. Here are a couple of ideas.

BLOODY MARY (SERVES SIX)
litre/22 fluid ounces of tomato juice
freshly squeezed lemons
freshly squeezed orange
25ml (4fl oz) vodka (adjust according to the strength of the vodka)
small wine glass *amontillado* sherry
Tabasco sauce to taste
Worcestershire sauce to taste
Celery salt to taste
ce

Horseradish or dill weed may be added, but can be considered a bit faddy and are not for purists.

If the situation is desperate and the idea of solids makes you shudder, the addition of a tin of beef bouillon to the Bloody Mary mixture (and the omission of the orange juice) converts the drink into a Bull's-eye, which should provide the nourishment you need until your stomach decides to be a touch more co-operative.

HEART STARTER
A little gin
Water
Liver Salts

Identical in appearance to a gin and tonic, especially after the addition of a slice of lemon (Vitamin C), and remarkably effective.

UNDERBERG
Evil-tasting bitters to be used in dire emergencies only...

...aejo 49
Alicante 47,104
Aloxe-Corton 12
Alsace 9,98,111,115,117,118
Alto Adige 33–4,111,115,116
Amontillado 93
Anjou 16,17,110
Apulia 38–9
Argentina 71,97,100,102, 103, 104,105,107,110, 111
Asti 36–7,116
Auckland 86,87
Baden 29,117
Bairrada 50,51
Bandol 19,104
Banyuls 22,96
Barbaresco 36–7,105
Bardolino 33–4
Barolo 36–7, 105
Barossa Valley 82,84,96, 101,111,114
Barsac 10,11,112,114
Basilicata 38,39
Beaujolais 12,13
Beaune 12,98
Bergerac 23,95
Bianco di Custoza 33
Blanc de blancs 15,109
Blanc de noirs 15,98
Blanquette de Limoux 22
Blaye 97,104
Bordeaux 10–11,95,102, 104, 105,112,114
Bourg 97, 104
Bourgueil 17, 102
Bourgogne 12–13,16,115,117
Brazil 75,102,110
British Columbia 69,115
Brouilly 13
Brunello di Montalcino 31,100
Bual 89
Burgundy 12–13,98,109, 115,117
Buzet 23,95
Cabernet d'Anjou 17,102
Cahors 23,104
Calabria 38,39
California 63–6,95,96,97, 98, 100,101,102,103, 104,105, 106,107,109, 110,111,112, 114,115, 116,117,119
Campania 38,39
Carmignano 31
Carneros 63
Casablanca Valley 72,74
Cassis 19,104
Catalonia 41,107
Cava 41
Central Otago 86,87,98
Chablis 12,13,109
Champagne 15,98,106,109
Châteauneuf-du-Pape 21,96, 101,104,118
Chénas 13
Chianti 31–2,100,119

Chile 72,74,103,104,105, 109, 110,111,115,117
Chinon 17,102
Chiroubles 13
Cirò 38
Clare Valley 84,111
Claret 10
Clos de Vougeot 98
Condrieu 20
Coonawarra 82,84,95,101
Corbières 22,103,104
Cornas 20,101
Corton 98
Corton-Charlemagne 12,109
Costers del Segre 41,107
Côte de Beaune 12
Côte de Brouilly 13
Côte Chalonnaise 12
Côte de Nuits 12
Côte d'Or 12
Côte-Rôtie 20,101,119
Coteaux d'Aix-en-Provence 19
Coteaux du Languedoc 22
Coteaux du Layon 16,17,110
Coteaux du Tricastin 21
Côtes de Bordeaux 11
Côtes de Castillon 11
Côtes du Frontonnais 23
Côtes de Gascogne, Vin de Pays des 23,119
Côtes de Provence 19,104
Côtes du Rhône 21,96, 104
Côtes du Roussillon 22,104
Côtes du Ventoux 21,96
Crémant 9
Crozes-Hermitage 20,101, 118
Crusted Port 91
Curicó Valley 72,74
Dão 50,51
Dealul Mare 59
Dôle 60
Douro 50, 51
Eden Valley 84,111
Emilia-Romagna 32, 95, 97, 100,102
Entre-Deux-Mers 11,112
Faugères 22
Fino sherry 93
Fitou 22, 103
Fleurie 13
Franciacorta 37
Franken 29,118
Frascati 31, 119
Friuli-Venezia Giulia 33, 34, 97,111
Fronsac 11,97
Fumé Blanc 112
Gaillac 23
Gattinara 36,105
Gavi 36
Gevrey-Chambertin 12,98
Ghemme 36,105
Gigondas 21, 96
Gisborne 86,87,115
Givry 12
Graves 10,11,95
Haut-Médoc 11
Hawke's Bay 86,87,110
Hermitage 20,101,118
Hock 26

Hunter Valley 81,101,114
Icewine 111
Idaho 67
Juliénas 13
Jumilla 47
Jura 23,98
Jurançon 23
Klein Karoo 78
Lacryma Christi del Vesuvio 38,39
Lambrusco 31,32
Languedoc 22,95,103,118,119
Late Bottled Vintage Port 91
Latium 32,100
Liebfraumilch 26,28,116
Liguria 37
Limoux 22
Liqueur Muscat 81
Lirac 21,96
Loire 16–17,95,98,102, 104, 110,112,117
Lombardy 37,102
Loupiac 112
Lugana 37
McLaren Vale 84
Mâcon 12,109
Mâcon-Lugny 12
Mâconnais 12
Madeira 89
Madiran 23
Maipo Valley 72
Málaga 47
Malmsey 89
Mancha, La 42,96,107
Manzanilla 93
Marches 32,100
Margaret River 85
Margaux 10,11
Marlborough 86,87,111,112
Marsala 38,39
Martinborough 86,87,98
Maule Valley 72,74
Médoc 10, 11, 95, 112
Menetou-Salon 16,17,112
Mercurey 12
Meritage 63,95,102,114
Meursault 12,109
Mexico 75,103,110,117,119
Minervois 22,103
Mittelrhein 26,28
Monbazillac 23,112
Montagny 12
Montepulciano d'Abruzzo 31,32
Monterey 63,111
Montilla-Moriles 47
Montrachet 12,109
Morey-St-Denis 12
Morgon 13
Moscatel de Setúbal 49
Moscato d'Asti 12
Mosel 26,28
Moulin-à-Vent 13
Muscat de Beaumes-de-Venise 21,116
Muscat de Frontignan 22
Muscat de Mireval 22
Muscat de Rivesaltes 22,96
Muscadet 16,17
Nahe 26,28
Napa Valley 63,66,95,100, 114

Navarra 43,96,107
New South Wales (NSW) 81,114
New York 68,102,109,111
Niersteiner 28
Nuits-St-Georges 12,98
Oloroso 93
Ontario 69,111
Oregon 67,98,109,111, 115,117
Orvieto 31,32,119
Paarl 77,78
Pacific Northwest 67,114
Padthaway 84
Pale cream sherry 93
Palo Cortado 93
Pauillac 10,11
Pedro Ximénez 93
Penedès 41,96,107
Pernand-Vergelesses 12
Peru 75
Pessac-Léognan 112,114
Pfalz 26,28,111,117
Piemonte 36–7,95,102,105
Piesport 25
Pomerol 10,11,97
Pommard 12
Port 79,90–1,107
Pouilly-Fuissé 12,109
Pouilly-Fumé 16,17,112
Premières Côtes de Bordeaux 11
Priorato 41,96
Prosecco 33
Provence 19,103
Puglia see Apulia
Puligny-Montrachet 12
Queensland 85
Quincy 16,17,112
Rapel Valley 72
Rasteau 96
Reciото 34
Regnié 13
Retsina 57
Reuilly 16,17,112
Rheinhessen 26,28
Rheinpfalz see Pfalz
Rheingau 26,28,111
Rhine 26,28
Rhône 20–1,96,101,104, 116,118,119
Rias Baixas 44
Ribatejo 49
Ribeiro 44
Ribera del Duero 46,107
Rioja 43,96,103,107
Romanée-Conti 98
Rosé d'Anjou 16
Rosé de la Loire 17
Rosso di Montalcino 31–2
Roussillon 22,96,103,118,119
Ruby port 90
Rueda 46
Rully 12
Ruwer 25,111
Saale-Unstrut 29
Saar 25,111
Sachsen 29
St-Amour 13
St-Chinian 22
St-Emilion 10,11,97,102
St-Estèphe 10–11

St-Joseph 20,101,118
St-Julien 10,11
St-Péray 20,118
St-Véran 12
Salice Salentino 39
Sancerre 16,17,98,112
Sardinia 38,39
Saumur 17,110
Saumur-Champigny 17
Sauternes 10,11,112,114
Savennières 16,17,110
Savoie 23,118
Sekt 26
Sercial 89
Sherry 93
Sicily 38,39
Single Quinta Port 91
Soave 33,117,119
Somontano 43,107
Sonoma 63,114
Spanna 36,105
Stellenbosch 77,78
Super Tuscans 31,32,95, 97,100
Swan Valley 85
Tarragona 41,96
Tasmania 85
Tavel 21,96
Tawny port 90
Tokaji 58
Tokay 58,81
Torgiano 32
Toro 46,107
Touraine 16,110,112
Trás-os-Montes 50
Trentino-Alto Adige 33–4, 97, 111,116
Tuscany 31–2,100,118,119
Umbria 32,100
Uruguay 75,102,103,117
Vacqueyras 21
Valais 60,117
Valdeorras 44
Valdepeñas 42,107
Valencia 47,104
Valle d'Aosta 37
Valpolicella 33–4
Vaud 60
Vega Sicilia 46,96,107
Veneto 33–4,97
Verdelho 89
Verdicchio 31,119
Vermentino 37
Vernaccia di San Gimignano 31–2
Victoria 81,98,115
Vin jaune 23
Vin santo 32
Vinho Verde 50,51
Vino Nobile di Montepulciano 31–2,100
Vintage champagne 15
Vintage port 90–1
Volnay 12
Vosne-Romanée 12
Vouvray 16,17,110
Washington 67,97,102, 111,114,115
Western Australia 85,98
White Port 91
White Zinfandel 63,66,107
Württemberg 29,111,117
Yarra Valley 81